MW01620590

Studio Aisberg

האקליפטוס
The Eucalyptus
ARTISTS COLONY
חוצות היוצר

Chef

The Eucalyptus Cookbook

Moshe Basson

With Sharon Fradis

Foreword by Claudia Roden

Levin Press

Foreword
by Claudia Roden

I got to know Moshe Basson more than thirty years ago when I was taken by an Israeli friend to his restaurant, a hut with a eucalyptus tree growing through it, in an industrial district of Jerusalem. The food was pure joy and I never forgot the experience. All that I tasted had been prepared in the refined way Jews had cooked at home in parts of the Middle East. When Moshe came out of the kitchen, my friend told him I was a food writer and gave him my name. He hugged me and rushed back into the kitchen to fetch my book. He made us taste a whole lot more dishes that kept coming. I remember them still – a delicately flavored soup with dumplings; stuffed vegetables; fried kubbeh with a very fine crisp meaty shell and a deliciously aromatic filling; and, the famous Palestinian makloubeh. Moshe said the balouza, a rose scented jelly, was my recipe to which he had added his rose petal jam.

I see Moshe every time I go to Jerusalem. It is always a great pleasure and exciting, and I learn something new. We've picked wild herbs on the Jerusalem hills. We've shopped in the Mahane Yehuda Market in Jerusalem. I've eaten in his home when his mother cooked the dishes of her family in Iraq. He introduced me to his Arab colleagues, members of the Artists for Peace organization of which he is one of the founders. One of the things you notice about his restaurants is the harmony that reigns between Muslims, Christians, and Jews who cook together and wait at tables.

Over the years, I've enjoyed fabulous food at his restaurants – both classic dishes from all over the Jewish diaspora, and his own unique interpretations. I remember a magnificent Moroccan cigar of duck and figs accompanied by a vanilla carrot puree and pumpkin jam, a lamb with dates, and a savory lentil stew. I love the way he combines flavors and textures and the way he marries ingredients, which are surprising and yet, nostalgic, triggering almost forgotten memories.

In 2017, when I was in Israel for a conference, Moshe gave a party that I will never forget. It was at The Eucalyptus restaurant in the Artists Colony at the foot of the Old City walls. The tables were set out in the street. He had invited friends – chefs and food writers. He said that to honor me he had taken dishes from my book and made them with a twist. Everyone was delighted and I was enthralled.

Introduction

Often, I'm asked about the origins of my cooking and cuisine. I'm taken back to my first cooking memory. As a small boy, I remember several occasions in which my mom longingly reminisced about eggs cooked in a bonfire. She said that those were the most tasty eggs she'd ever eaten. She told me how they cooked them on some mornings in a charcoal grill that they used to heat the kettle, back in Iraq, where she grew up. She moved to Israel when she was seventeen, with me, a ten-month-old baby in her arms.

One day, my sister and I were left alone, and we played in our backyard in the Talpiot neighborhood of Jerusalem. I remember digging a small waterfall with a miniature brook and setting seashells to decorate it. Then we built a bonfire and I took eggs from our free-range chicken and put the first egg in the fire. It exploded. I put in the second egg, and it exploded too. As the bonfire died out, I placed the remaining eggs there and forgot all about them, moving on to other games. When my mother returned, she picked up the scent of the cooked eggs, and came to hug me for cooking the eggs for her and bringing her memories to life. That made me realize that the eggs should actually be cooked on a bed of ember, not in the bonfire, and later on, when I grew up, I also realized there's a special link between food and memories.

Our eucalyptus tree was planted on Tu B'Shvat – the Jewish New Year of the Trees – during the full moon of February, the perfect time to plant trees. I wanted to plant a small eucalyptus near our home. My father was dismayed. He said that I should plant a fruit-bearing tree endemic to the land of Israel. I argued that I felt a strong attachment to this tree. He finally agreed, reassuring himself by reciting the Talmudic promise that in the future (when the Messiah will come), all the trees in Israel would bear fruit. Talmud Ketubot 112b:3.

Little did we know that this specific tree was not an ordinary eucalyptus. It did in fact bear fruit – The

Eucalyptus restaurant grew under its leaves. Since I established the restaurant in 1986, just outside my first childhood home, I have been grooming and pampering this little fruit that has brought so much joy. It has become my goal to have people visit the restaurant to experience the Land of Israel cuisine.

To garner this cuisine, I have looked deep into the past. Not only to my personal history, but to our collective past, to the people of the Land of Israel of all religions and cultures. I embarked on the study of ancient texts – a most fascinating look into the life and eating habits of our forebearers in this region. I discovered magnificent wild herbs and plants, ways to find them and prepare them. I used for inspiration the wonderful traditional Arabic dishes cooked by our neighbors of my childhood, as well as the Iraqi dishes prepared by my mother, my grandmothers, and my aunts.

In The Eucalyptus kitchen, together with my son, Ronny, we bring a modern Israeli interpretation to the Land of Milk and Honey with food from the Bible.

Of Salt and Precision

For my dear mother Spirons Basson, with love and adoration. Thank you for the love seasoned with curiosity and knowledge of food that you have instilled in me from infancy to the present day.

Moshe Basson

For many years now, I have been cooking my mother's tomato-mint soup. I must have cooked it a thousand times, and I guess that by now I have even made it more times than she has. Still, it never tastes the same as hers. And yet, she cooks without even tasting the soup and her tomato-mint soup is a constant flavor in our life.

When I cook, I need to taste the soup again and again at the fine-tuning stage. I add some lemon and I taste, I add a pinch of salt and taste again. And again, I add lemon juice, salt or sugar and taste.

One time, I found myself adding salt from the palm of my hand. I like to use this "measurement." Then, I added a palmful again without tasting and without a conscious thought. Immediately after, I scolded myself for being absent-minded and not tasting and reminded myself to stay alert when cooking. But, to my surprise it tasted good.

When it happened again, I started analyzing the mechanism behind the process.

Working in the kitchen, simmering broths and sautéing fresh garlic and greens, our nose constantly picks up scents – odor molecules – and transfers them on a direct pathway to the amygdala, the emotional ground control of our brain. The associative learning between smell and behavioral responses takes place in the amygdala. And my theory of cooking without tasting relies mainly on that connection. The aromas of the stew enter our nose, activating memories of past times, and we compare smells and adjust seasonings, almost automatically.

Modern life has gradually deprived our society of the need, and subsequently, the trust, of using our senses. This is especially true of the sense of smell. In ancient times the opposite was true: the olfactory sense was very critical, a matter of life and death.

I believe that a good cook has a good memory. I believe that my mother's way of cooking is primarily about the memory of scents, and the comparison is done by feedback mechanism. A signal is sent to the hand: add more lemon, add some mint. The signal manifests in the form of palmful quantities, and not in pounds or ounces. It made me realize how grandmothers were able to produce the same flavors even if the tomatoes were sour at times or bland at the end of the season. In our family, we have a wonderful cook who does not eat any garlic or onions, but still manages to cook with these ingredients and produce great dishes. Many vegetarians cooking meat for their family become masters of sniffing out flavors.

When we build a recipe, it is relatively easy to instruct that two carrots should be added or to give the amount of rice in cups or grams. However, the more elusive entity is the seasoning.

Changes in seasoning are required as a result of differences in ingredients. Produce tend to have varying flavors depending on the season and on their source. When we cook, we need to take into account all these parameters and adjust.

There is a simple and fun experiment I like: set two cups of coffee on the table, one with two teaspoons of sugar. Try to tell which is which based only on its aroma.

I encourage you to trust your instinct, or, to be precise, your nose, when you cook. Allow your own sense of taste and smell guide you through the process.

Vegetables

Fattoush Salad

By Bread Alone

My father, whom I loved dearly, was a man of faith. He was committed to the Jewish schedule of prayers, and adhered to the Jewish faith's commands. His regard for bread fit into that sacred space.

His regard for bread may have been the result of the juxtaposition of his own beginnings in the family bakery and the strong presence of bread in the Bible, which he read over and over again. That monumental status of bread meant that whenever he saw some castaway bread lying on the ground, he would pick it up and kiss it, gently laying it above the ground.

Growing up in Israel's austerity and rationing years, where you had trouble sourcing egg powder, let alone an actual egg, had an immense affect on my mentality for years. There were other years though, when waste meant plenty and a lifestyle of comfort. Now, there is a blessed full circle return to sanity with regard to waste and people are more conscious about their consumption.

Bread has followed the trends of food conservation in general, but it also has a special status. For instance, it has held a sacred place in religious ceremonies for Judaism and Christianity. There are even dishes that make use of stale bread in many cultures.

In ancient Judaic worship, the showbread, *lehem hapanim*, was always present on the dedicated table in the Temple of Jerusalem. There were special regulations for the amount of flour and salt that were to be used, and there was a specification for a cup of frankincense on top of the showbread pile.

Christianity has Communion bread eaten at Mass and for many Christians bread represents the embodiment of Jesus. The miracle of the loaves and fishes attested to Jesus's ability to feed the multitudes with just a few loaves and two fish.

Fattoush salad, like panzanella salad and like French toast, is one of these "economical-turns-favorite" dishes, which originated from a need to find use for stale bread, and became a lot more than a compromise. And that is the genius of a good cook.

Serves 4

3 pita breads, about 6½ oz / 180 g
1 tbsp olive oil
½ tsp salt
1 tsp za'atar spice blend
3 tomatoes
3 cucumbers, very fresh
2 radishes
3-4 sprigs green onions
1 cup torn romaine lettuce
5 sprigs fresh mint, coarsely chopped
½ cup arugula
1 scant tsp sea salt
3 tsp sumac
2 tbsp freshly squeezed lemon juice
3 tbsp olive oil

Break the pita bread into pieces ⅔ inch / 1½ cm in size.
Heat the olive oil in a pan over medium heat, and add the pita bread cubes. Spread the salt and za'atar, tossing frequently until the pita has browned.
Allow to cool.
Dice the vegetables into pieces ⅔ inch / 1½ cm in size.
Place vegetables and pita bread in a large serving bowl and add salt, sumac, lemon juice, and olive oil. Mix well to combine the flavors.

Fire-Charred Eggplant in Raw Tahini and Pomegranate Syrup

Some dishes are born out of an experiment. In those cases, we gradually develop a new combination of flavors, serve it to a trustworthy crowd, and adjust it over time. And then we have those occasions that demonstrate that necessity is indeed the mother of invention.

During those first years in Talpiot, when the tree for which The Eucalyptus was named and around which its rooftop was built had just topped the ceiling, most of our dishes were traditional Jerusalem cooking. We had our tomato-mint kubbeh, hummus salad, and of course, the beloved Middle Eastern eggplant salad, baba ganoush.

In those days, we also had some regular customers. Our waitstaff had memorized their usual order and would place it as soon as they saw the customer

walking in the door, both to expedite the process and secure their tips.

One afternoon, our veteran waitress spotted a customer coming in whose favorite dish was baba ganoush. She immediately rushed to the kitchen to order the dish and was mortified to discover we had run out of it.

That day I was cooking at the grill station that was located in the dining room. The waitress came over to alert me that we had run out of eggplant salad, that the cook had insisted he had no time to make it during the lunch rush, and that we may have an unhappy customer. *Tell him to make it*, she urged.

I asked her to get me two eggplants, and I placed them on the grill. That was same station where we prepared the date honey (silan) and raw tahini dessert plate, so I had squeeze bottles of both on hand. Once the eggplant was charred and ready, I peeled it and placed it whole on one of the dessert plates, crushing it a bit with a knife. I seasoned it lightly with salt and lemon juice, drizzled from the squeeze bottles some raw tahini and a bit of silan, and then finished with a sprinkling of chopped parsley.

When the waitress reached for my ready-to-serve invention, she was very skeptical and reluctant, saying it wasn't baba ganoush and the patron wouldn't like it. To her surprise, he was thrilled with the new take on his favorite.

As time passed, we conducted some trials. The general notion was to eliminate the sweet and heavier silan and replace it with pomegranate syrup which lightens up the tahini and adds wonderful tartness. In season, we sprinkle it with fresh pomegranate seeds which give it beautiful specks of ruby and a sweet and sour crunch.

Serves 4

2 medium sized eggplants

½ cup raw tahini (can be purchased in Middle Eastern food stores)

2 tablespoons fresh lemon juice

¼ cup pomegranate syrup

salt to taste

½ cup pomegranate seeds

¼ cup fresh chopped parsley

There are 3 options for roasting the eggplants:

The recommended options are either over charcoal, or using a gas range or cooktop, so that the eggplant has a smoky flavor. If using the gas range, cover the base of the burners with aluminum foil. Roast the eggplants on medium flames for about 20 minutes. Rotate, using tongs, every 3 minutes. The eggplants should be completely charred.

A third option is to heat the oven to 450°F / 230°C. Place a baking pan under the top rack. Make a few pin holes in the eggplants to allow the vapors out and place the eggplants on the top rack under the broiler. Rotate every 5 minutes until blackened, about 30 minutes.

Remove from heat and allow to cool.

Peel the charred skin off using your fingers, do not use water to wash skin away. Little bits of char left on the eggplant is fine.

Let excess liquids drip out of the eggplants. Keep the stem of the eggplants on for serving.

Place the eggplants on a serving dish and slightly mash the flesh of the eggplant with a knife or spoon, while keeping the shape of the eggplant intact.

Season with salt and a little lemon juice.

Spoon some raw tahini on top and then drizzle with aged pomegranate syrup (you can also reduce pomegranate juice with sugar for the same effect).

Decorate with pomegranate seeds and chopped parsley.

Serve immediately.

Fried Cauliflower with Tomato Cream

The Crunchy Fractal

This cauliflower dish is somewhat surprising, as people don't expect to get enthusiastic over cauliflower. The fried cauliflower has a completely unexpected texture and people often think we have processed it in some special way. It has a crunchy quality on the outside, yet it is not breaded, and on the inside, it is both soft and has a bit of a bite. *Did you sous vide the cauliflower?* This is one question we have been asked while a baffled guest tried to identify the cooking process. We answer in the negative.

When accompanied with the delectable duo of tomato and tahini, it becomes addictive. It is one of the dishes for which we most often get requests for seconds (and thirds) when people dine on the tasting menu.

Cauliflower is a bit of a disputed vegetable in Israel. Its shape and the fact that it grows so close to the ground make it very hard to keep pests away and to properly wash it to remove any possible "visitors." Some rabbis have considered disallowing it altogether from the lexicon of permitted foods, claiming it is impossible to check it thoroughly and ensure it abides by strict kosher-law regulations.

However, where humans fail, machines prevail. Some very crafty assembly lines have been constructed in Israel specifically to keep up with the cauliflower demand. First the cauliflower are broken into florets, then they go through a jet stream that removes any impurities by sheer force of wind, they then enter a bath of agitating water to get thoroughly cleaned, then are briefly cooked, and finally, they are frozen. While this process seems quite extreme to someone who is used to simply cutting up and cooking their store-bought produce, this is the method that allows us and many other kosher restaurants to keep serving this incredible vegetable.

And we are lucky that the brief cooking the kosher cauliflower undergoes does wonders for its texture.

Serves 6

4 cups / 1 liter water

2 lb / 900 g cauliflower, broken into small florets

500 ml canola oil for deep frying

salt

2 tsp sumac

2 tbsp lemon juice

6 tbsp tahini sauce, plus extra to serve (recipe below).

Boil the water in a medium saucepan and cook the cauliflower in 3 batches, each for about 3 minutes.
Drain and set aside.
Pour the oil into a large saucepan and place over medium-high heat. Heat the oil until it reaches 350°F / 175°C – when a wooden spoon is inserted, bubbles form around it. Using tongs, carefully place into the oil a few florets at a time. Cook until golden brown, for about 5 minutes. Drain on paper towels. Repeat with the rest of the cauliflower florets.
Place the fried cauliflower in a mixing bowl and add salt, sumac, and lemon juice. Mix in the tahini and add 9 tablespoons of tomato salsa (recipe below), and 6 tablespoons of tomato cream (recipe below). Allow to sit for about 10 minutes.
To serve, spread tomato cream on a serving dish and place a heap of cauliflower on top. Drizzle with tahini. See below for tomato cream, tomato salsa, and tahini recipes.

Tomato Cream

2 cloves garlic, finely chopped

1 tbsp olive oil

7 oz / 200 g canned tomatoes

salt

black pepper

¼ tsp turmeric

¼ tsp fresh thyme or hyssop

¼ tsp sugar

Place all the ingredients in a small saucepan and bring to a boil over medium heat. Decrease the heat to medium-low and cook for about 10 minutes. Using a food processor or a blender, process until smooth.

Tomato Salsa

1 clove garlic

¼ small red chile to taste

1 tbsp olive oil

6 oz / 170 g ripe tomatoes

¼ cup cilantro

1 tbsp lemon juice

½ tsp salt

½ tsp ground coriander seeds

Place all the ingredients in a food processor and pulse until the sauce is coarsely chopped, not smooth.

Tahini Sauce

¾ cup light tahini paste

½ cup water

2 tbsp freshly squeezed lemon juice

salt

Shake the tahini paste container vigorously before pouring the tahini, blending the paste together.

Whisk the tahini and water in a medium bowl for about 4 minutes until a smooth creamy consistency is achieved. Add the lemon juice and salt and mix. The amount of water and salt is very dependent on the consistency of the tahini paste. The sauce should be runny and delicate in flavor.

Tabbouleh

Parched by the Sun

It's fascinating to find evidence of unadorned day-to-day living in the Bible. In the epic scene of the rebellion of Absalom against his own father, King David, the rebels gather in an assembly. Absalom seeks the counsel of Achitophel, the advisor of King David, who has already betrayed the King. Achitophel gives Absalom good advice. Nonetheless, Absalom rejects that good advice and instead accepts the advice of Hushai, the double agent loyal to King David. Waiting close by, Jonathan and Ahimaaz receive word to warn King David, but in the meantime they are discovered by a boy loyal to Absalom and they must hide.

They escape to the home of a man living in the town of Bahurim. That man has a well in his courtyard and into that well they descend. The woman of the house smoothly takes a cloth and covers the well. She then spreads grains on the cloth to dry in the sun and *nothing was known of it.* 2 Samuel 17:19.

This process of partially cooking the wheat, then spreading it to dry in the sun before cracking it into coarse or fine bulgur was so commonplace that it served as the perfect camouflage for King David's men hiding in the well. To this day, following the wheat harvest season in Arab villages, the fellahs, the farmers, still use this ancient technique to produce bulgur.

Serves 4

½ cup fine bulgur wheat
1 cup hot water
4 green onions, thinly sliced
1½ cups parsley, finely chopped
⅔ cup mint leaves, finely chopped
1 tomato, finely chopped
½ tsp salt
⅓ cup lemon juice
⅓ cup olive oil
½ cup pomegranate seeds, or 2 tbsp pomegranate molasses

Place the bulgur with the hot water in a mixing bowl. Leave to soak for about 10 minutes. Drain and cool.
Mix together all the ingredients by lightly fluffing with a fork, making sure not to compress the salad in any way. It should be light and airy.
Adjust seasoning.

YONATAN'S FARMS LTD

لبن مخيض
انتاج شركة الجنيدي
AL JUNEIDI

Mushroom Stuffed "Candies"

Makes about 40 parcels

For the dough:

2 cups / 250 g all-purpose flour

¼ tbsp salt

½ tbsp sugar

½ cup / 125 ml tepid water

1½ tbsp vegetable oil

To make the dough:

In a mixer, mix all the dry ingredients and add the water and oil. Knead on a low setting for 5 minutes or until the texture of the dough is super smooth and elastic. Set to rest for 20 minutes.

For the filling:

1 onion, finely diced

1 large clove garlic, minced

9 oz / 250 g oyster mushrooms, roughly chopped

1 tsp fresh thyme

olive oil

For the garnish:

4 tbsp amba aioli (page 224)

1 cup almond labane (page 222)

To make the filling:

In a large pan, add olive oil to coat the bottom of the pan and sauté the onions to golden brown. Add the mushrooms and continue to sauté until they lose their moisture, add the garlic, thyme, nutmeg, salt, and pepper. Let the mixture cool completely. To assemble the parcels:

Cut dough into small pieces and roll out to small circles. The dough should be about ¼ inch / ½ cm thick so that it does not tear when filling and folding.

Spoon in the filling into the center, leaving space on the edges to fold.

Fold into an envelope, and pinch the edges together, so you get a neat little square.

Bake at 375°F / 190°C until golden brown, about 15 minutes.

Serve warm with a dollop of almond labane, and drizzle with amba aioli.

Purslane with Tahini

Foraging the Backyard – Common Purslane

There is an interesting irony common to many of the backyard forageable plants. While they are virtually everywhere, growing in abundance without being planted, their remarkable nutritious level puts them on par with select leafy green superfoods. It is as if the universe takes personal care of our diet; but people have difficulty looking at these wonderful plants as food.

Purslane is one of these magnificent plants. In fact, it is so common, it is one of eight of the most common plant species in the world. Scientists have traced the plant from North Africa to North America, and in my imagination, it is as if an angel was holding a fistful of seeds and sprinkling them on Mediterranean ground.

Purslane can be eaten raw, and we like to add it to our Eucalyptus salad. It can be stir fried and makes a great addition to omelettes. The entire plant can be eaten, and it is a rich source for omega 3 and potassium.

Rabbi Yehudah HaNasi called it *halaglogot*. There is a short anecdote in the Jerusalem Talmud in which the sages could not identify the meaning of several Hebrew words including *halaglogot*. They went to the famous Rabbi Yehuda's home, where a maid instructed them on how to enter respectfully. In the meantime, one of them dropped the purslane he was holding. The maid offered to sweep up the "*halaglogot*." So, she solved the mystery for the rabbis and for all posterity. Jerusalem Talmud, Megilla 18:26.

Serves 2

14 oz / 400 g purslane or wild mallow or spinach
4 tbsp olive oil
5 cloves garlic, sliced
½ tsp black pepper
2 sprigs thyme
½ tsp salt
1 tsp sumac (optional)

½ cup / 120 ml tahini sauce (page 225)

Wash the purslane leaves thoroughly and pat dry.
Heat the oil in a large frying pan on medium heat. Add the garlic and cook for about 4-5 minutes until golden. Add the purslane and seasonings and stir. Cook for about 10 minutes, stirring continuously.
Serve in a small heap topped with 1½ tablespoons of tahini.

Patatas Bravas

Melting pots make fertile beds for cultivating new dishes, or new takes on traditional ones. Fusion cuisines inspire endless combinations which produce great innovations. Sometimes an ingredient or a dish goes there and back again to reach fame.

The patatas bravas dish is essentially a famous Spanish tapas dish which traveled the world as a tapas bar regular. It made its way into the restaurant's menu via several connections.

Jerusalem's importance to Christians is well established, thus pilgrims from many different places come to Jerusalem to connect to their religious past. It is a privilege to host these special dinner events for pilgrims from all around the world, to be able to take part in the meaningful emotional and history-rich journey, and to manifest both aspects of the visit with dishes inspired by the Bible.

One day, our marketing director and customer service manager, Michal and Sharbel, were brainstorming for additions to the dinner menu for a Spanish pilgrims group. Having been raised in Chicago, Michal had frequented a beloved Spanish tapas bar that served the famous patatas bravas dish. She suggested that we make our version of it.

It was an immediate hit. We coupled the beautifully crispy potatoes with roasted duck slices, and it became an honored item on the menu.

Serves 4 as a starter

For the potatoes:

6 Yukon gold potatoes

olive oil

For the sauce:

½ cup aioli

1 heaping tbsp tomato paste

3 tbsp red wine vinegar

salt

pepper

1 tbsp quality smoked paprika

a pinch of cayenne, optional

5⅓ oz / 150 g duck confit, cut into bite-size chunks, optional

To make the potatoes:

Preheat the oven to 400°F / 200°C.

Place the potatoes on the middle rack and bake until a fork slides in easily, about 40 minutes.

Remove and let cool for 10 minutes.

Cut the potatoes into bite size chunks.

Pour enough olive oil into a large frying pan to come up ¼ inch / ½ cm, and heat over medium-high heat.

Cook the potato chunks in batches in the oil until golden and crisp, about 8 minutes.

Set to drain over a colander.

To make the sauce:

Mix the ingredients for the sauce in a medium mixing bowl and set in the refrigerator for about 2 hours to rest and merge flavors.

To assemble the patatas bravas:

Place the potatoes in a large serving bowl and add the sauce, blending well.

Place the duck chunks over the patatas bravas.

Stuffed Jerusalem Sage Leaves

Makes about 60 sage rolls

60 sage leaves

For the filling:

1½ cups white rice, rinsed
1½ onions, finely chopped
½ cup fresh mint, leaves and soft sprigs, finely chopped
½ cup fresh parsley, leaves and soft sprigs, finely chopped
½ cup fresh celery, leaves and soft sprigs, finely chopped
2 tomatoes, finely chopped
¾ tsp thyme
½ tsp black pepper
½ tsp ground nutmeg
½ tsp ground allspice
1½ tsp salt
1½ tbsp freshly squeezed lemon juice
⅓ cup olive oil
2 cups white button mushrooms, diced into ½ inch / 1 cm cubes OR ⅔ lb / 300 g ground beef

For the base:

3 potatoes, peeled and cut into ¼ inch / ½ cm slices
15 garlic cloves
½ tsp salt
¼ cup olive oil

Place a large pot with plenty of water on high heat and bring to a boil.
Soak the sage leaves in batches of 20 in the water for 3 minutes.

If using the mushroom option, heat ½ tbsp olive oil over medium-high heat, and sauté the mushrooms for 5 minutes, stirring occasionally. Remove from heat.

Place all the ingredients for the filling in a large mixing bowl, and blend well.
Layer a stockpot with potato slices.

Spread a sage leaf on a cutting board, shiny side down. Take a teaspoonful of the filling and gently place on the bottom end of the leaf.
Fold the sides over the filling, pressing gently. The filling should be neatly covered, but not too tightly so it will have room to absorb liquids when cooked.
Roll up the leaf from the bottom up in a tight roll.
Place the leaf on top of the potatoes. Repeat with the rest of the leaves.
Place 3-4 garlic cloves between layers.
Once all the leaves are nicely rolled and sitting snugly in the pot, add water, just covering the rolls, and add salt, and olive oil.
Cover with a layer of torn leaves, cover the pot with a heatproof plate on top of the rolls. Simmer for about 30 minutes. The liquid should be absorbed.
Allow to sit for 10 minutes before uncovering.

Red Shakshuka

Serves 3-6

1 tbsp olive oil
1 medium onion, coarsely chopped
3 cloves garlic, finely sliced
1 medium sweet red pepper, seeded and diced into 2×1 inch / 1×1½ cm pieces
2 tsp tomato paste (optional)
6 large ripe tomatoes, finely chopped
1½ tsp salt
½ tsp freshly ground black pepper
scant 1 tsp thyme / oregano / za'atar leaves
6 free-range eggs

Pour the olive oil into a sauté pan and place over medium heat.

Add the onions and cook till golden, add the garlic, red pepper and tomato paste and cook for 2 minutes.

Add the tomatoes and spices and cook for about 8 minutes, partially covered, occasionally stirring. Add salt to taste.

When the red pepper has softened, make 6 depressions in the sauce using the back of a ladle, and gently break an egg into each depression.

Cover the pan with a lid and cook for 3 minutes if you wish to have a runny yolk, or for 4 minutes more for a solid one.

You can also scramble the eggs, as did my mother-in-law to cook her Hungarian lecso recipe.

Serve with a freshly baked focaccia to soak up the richness.

Fried Eggplant

Look for the lightest, shiny, deep purple eggplants for this recipe; heavier eggplant means there are more seeds, which would mean more bitterness.

Serves 6

2 eggplants

course salt

vegetable oil, for frying

Stripe the eggplant lengthwise with a vegetable peeler and trim off the ends. Slice into ¾ inch / 1½ cm thick round slices, and set in a single layer on a tray. Sprinkle the eggplant slices on both sides with coarse salt. Leave to drain for about 40 minutes.

Discard the leftover salt, and pat the slices dry with a paper towel.

Pour enough oil into a large skillet to come up 1 inch / 2 cm, and place over medium-high heat. When the oil is hot, and bubbles form around the tip of a wooden spoon, fry the eggplant in batches for about 2-3 minutes per side, until golden. Using a spatula, transfer the eggplant to paper towels to drain.

Avocado Salad

Serves 6 as a starter

1 small onion, about 1⅔ oz / 50 g coarsely chopped

3 tbsp freshly squeezed lemon juice

3 large very ripe Hass avocados, about 1½ lb / 700 g in total

2½ oz / 70 g cilantro, coarsely chopped

1 tsp salt

In a food processor bowl, place the onion and add the lemon juice.

While the onion is marinating, peel the avocado, remove the core, and cut into 2 inch / 5 cm wedges.

Add the chopped cilantro to the food processor bowl and place the avocado wedges on top.

Sprinkle the salt and pulse to a coarse texture.

Minimize the processing – stop when it is barely blended to avoid blackening of the avocado.

Taste for salt and lemon and adjust.

The comforting chatter, the smell of another cup of coffee, the red diffusion of the hibiscus tea, and the occasional laughter fulfill my pursuit. In a way, this is the embodiment of, *Wherefore the children of Israel shall keep the Sabbath, to observe the Sabbath throughout their generations, for a perpetual covenant*.

Exodus 31:16.

Soups

Nettle Soup

Foraging the Backyard – Common Nettle

Nettles are an enchanted plant to me, and perhaps a misunderstood, unappreciated one. Hans Christian Andersen saw their enchantment and wove them into a fairy tale in which 11 scorned princes were turned into wild swans by the spell of an evil stepmother. They were saved by their princess sister who devotedly spun and knit 11 stinging nettle shirts to break the spell.

As a nine year old, gathering sorghum that had spilled from bags near the old rail station in Jerusalem, I wasn't very fond of nettles. Standing in my shorts in knee-high nettles that stung my over-sensitive skin, I leaned toward the biblical way of thinking: nettles were not greatly appreciated in the days of the Bible. The Bible refers to nettles and the wish that they were indeed replaced by myrtle: *Where once there were thorns, cypress trees will grow. Where nettles grew, myrtles will sprout up.* Isaiah 55:13.

Stinging nettle has a high mineral content and is rich in iron and protein which makes it great for treating anemia. Another interesting trait is its ability to counteract hay fever and allergies. There is an obvious paradox in the nettles causing infamous stings and itches, and nevertheless being able to treat the symptoms of these allergies.

When I started cooking with nettles, my first step was to make a nettle infusion drink, like an herbal tea, but it had some saltiness that made me think it would be better suited as a soup. I experimented with nettles and their texture after I became familiar with blanching mallow and spinach. To the nettles, I added vegetable stock, and enriched it with almond milk. The nettles have a rich nutty flavor, which complemented the almonds.

Years later, I discovered that from the same Scandinavian background as that of the fairy tale, there comes a Swedish nettle soup. That soup, usually served with hard boiled eggs, has a flavor and consistency very much along the same lines as my soup.

When we started serving the nettle soup in the restaurant, I talked to the diners about nettles and their great health benefits. From women native to Russia, I got the same response. They would groan and bemoan the time spent under the command of their babushkas (grandmothers) who made them sit for hours with their hair infused in nettle tea. I would always compliment their beautiful hair and encourage them to thank their grandmothers for a practice modern-day hair gurus still promote for hair strengthening.

If you can't source nettles, the best replacement is spinach, adding an addition of ½ cup of pecan nuts to the blanched almonds, and processing the pecans and almonds together before they are added to the soup.

Serves 6

1½ lb / 700 g fresh nettles
6 cups / 1½ liters water
2 cups blanched almonds
1 cup water
½ tbsp salt
¼ tsp freshly ground black pepper

Rinse the nettles carefully with cold water.
Pour the water in a stockpot and bring to a boil. Add a pinch of salt.
Blanch the nettles: place the nettles in the boiling water for 1 minute, then remove with tongs and put into a bowl of ice water.
Reserve the nettle water to use as stock.
Cut off the stringy part of the stalks and place the nettles in the stockpot with the hot water. On medium heat, simmer for about 20 minutes until soft, then use a stick blender to blend until the soup is smooth.
Place the almonds in a food processor with 1 cup of water. Process well until a thick paste forms and add to the soup.
Bring to a boil while mixing in the almond paste, cook for a few more minutes.
Season well with salt and pepper.

Grains and Beans

Focaccia

Masters of Our Planet

There's an old joke about dog owners. An extraterrestrial being studies the planet and concludes that dogs are the masters – they are looked after, fed, and walked in accordance with their routine, and the humble servants are their human caretakers.

Similarly, listening to the new historians, like Jared Diamond, the clear deduction is that grains are the rulers. Wheat is queen. Corn is king. Rice is the emperor. Out of all the flora, these grains have taken the land, and domesticated the humans, who, until they worked the agrarian farms, were hunting and gathering.

I often tell another story, that of a prehistoric man who frequents a wheat field to gather its raw berries. On one of his visits, lightning strikes and its fire starts consuming the man's precious food. He stands in awe and fear, and as the flames are waning, he smells for the first time the wonderful aroma of toasted wheat berries: the idea of cooking is born. That transformation of raw into baked wheat is another basis for civilization and a catalyst in the Neolithic revolution, pivoting the gatherers into settlers.

There are discussions and arguments over whether the individual was the main beneficiary of that change of direction, or whether that change caused society to gain the upper hand. As those questions beckon, we have breads and baked goods over which we can commune and comfort ourselves. So, let us eat focaccias.

Makes 8 servings

4 cups / 500 g all-purpose flour, sifted
½ tbsp sugar
scant ½ tbsp salt
¾ tbsp active dry yeast
4 tbsp / 50 ml olive oil
1¼ cups / 280 ml water
olive oil for brushing.
rosemary oil for brushing (page 227)

Place the dry ingredients in a large mixing bowl and stir. Pour in the olive oil and gradually add the water, combining with the dry ingredients.

Knead to a smooth dough, continue to knead for several minutes to achieve elastic consistency.

Add water if needed.

Form the dough into a ball and sprinkle with some flour, cover with a damp towel and allow to rest in a warm spot for about an hour or until it has doubled in size.

Preheat the oven to 450°F/ 230°C. If you have a baking stone, use it for best results.

Take out pieces of dough about 4 oz / 100 g in size. Shape into balls.

Line a baking sheet with parchment paper and set the dough balls to rise, covered with the damp towel for about 20 minutes.

Using your fingers, pull and stretch the dough balls in opposite directions to form a narrow rectangular shape, about 3 inches / 7 cm wide and 6 inches / 15 cm long, and arrange on a baking sheet.

Brush the focaccias with olive oil.

Bake for about 9 minutes until slightly golden.

Brush the baked focaccias with rosemary oil or plain olive oil.

Mallow Gnocchi

Foraging the Backyard – Common Mallow

You will find mallow growing in any patch where plants are allowed to grow wild. Sprouting out of a city sidewalk, flourishing in a forgotten garden bed, mallow doesn't require much to grow in abundance. While it is native to Europe, it can be found all over the world, spreading its opportunistic roots in various types of soil.

Mallow has many nicknames. The names usually derive from its flat round fruit and whatever food that shape resembles in a given locale or language. The sources of the nickname range from cheeses in Europe to challamit or chubeza in the Middle East. Challamit comes from the Hebrew, *challa*, the round braided Sabbath bread and the chubeza is from the Arabic *chubez*, meaning bread.

Mallow is high in nutrients and considered anti-inflammatory. The beloved marshmallow confection is a modern version of a 4000-year-old sore throat medicine originally made from the root of the marsh mallow plant. Mallow was known for being a survival food in times of famine, and it was the main ingredient in chubeza meatless meatballs in besieged Jerusalem in the 1948 war.

If you prefer foraging in the local supermarket, baby spinach would be an excellent replacement.

Serves 6

For the gnocchi:

1½ lb / 700 g potatoes

7 oz / 200 g mallow or spinach, stems and leaves

2 eggs

1¼ cups / 200 g all-purpose flour

1 tsp salt

For the tomato sauce:

4 tbsp olive oil

4 cloves garlic, thinly chopped

1 tsp fresh thyme leaves

14 oz / 400 g ripe or canned tomatoes

1 tsp salt

1 tsp sugar

1 tsp sweet paprika

lemon juice to taste

10 basil leaves

To make the gnocchi:

Place the potatoes in a pot and add water to cover by 1½ inches / 4 cm. Bring to a boil and cook for about 20 minutes, until a fork slides in easily. Drain and let dry.

Peel the potatoes and place in a large bowl, mash to a fine puree. You can use a ricer or a food mill, if you have one, though a potato masher is sufficient for the desired texture.

Place the mallow in a pot with boiling water for about 2 minutes until they wilt but still retain their color. Remove and place in a strainer to drain.

Transfer the mallow to a food processor, process until smooth, and then drain in a strainer again.

Beat the eggs and combine with the mallow.

Add the mallow mixture to the mashed potatoes, and add the flour, gently folding in. Continue to fold in until a soft dough texture is achieved. If the dough is sticky, add more flour in small amounts.

Transfer to a lightly floured board and divide the dough into 3 parts. Roll each part into a ¾ inch / 2 cm tube, and cut into 1 inch / 2½ cm gnocchi. Repeat with the rest of the dough.

Bring a large pot of water to a boil and sprinkle in some salt.

Gently place the gnocchi in the boiling water and cook for about 3 minutes until the gnocchi float to the surface. Drain and transfer to the tomato sauce.

To make the tomato sauce:

Heat the olive oil in a saucepan over medium-high heat, and add the garlic and thyme.

Add the tomatoes in 4 batches, allowing them to broil with the garlic.

Lower the heat to medium and add the salt, sugar, and sweet paprika as you stir.

Taste the sauce as tomatoes may taste from bland to sweet or sour, and add lemon juice up to 2 teaspoons. The sauce should be mildly sour.

Cook for about 15 minutes, stirring occasionally.

Chop the basil leaves and add to the saucepan.

Remove from heat.

Black-Eyed Peas Dip

Black-Eyed Peas Lucky Charms

Growing black-eyed peas is the national sport of my family. There is a non-declared contest of how long a pod one can grow. My sister hangs them on trellises to make an ornament out of the bright green pods, and then shows off their length.

When you grow black-eyed peas, you can have a taste of each stage of their growing cycle. When the pods are just starting, you can sacrifice some, and stir fry, or even cut them raw into the Eucalyptus Green Salad. As they mature, they can pose as string beans with great freshness and a nutty flavor, and eventually, when the pods are dried out and the peas shelled, they can be cooked as you would cook beans, without the need to soak them in advance.

The black-eyed peas' road to the New Year's table was paved with mistaken phonetic identities. Their Arabic and Hebrew name is *lubya*, which sounds like rubya, which in turn resembles *yirbu*, that is: will increase. The New Year blessing, *may it be that our merits increase*, puts pomegranate on the table, and for some Middle Eastern Jews, puts a dish of cooked green black-eyed pea pods, *lubya*, on the table as well. Some historians track the black-eyed peas all the way to the American South's New Year's table, where Sephardic Jewish colonists coming from Spain, brought the tradition with them. The southern dish comes in the form of dried black-eyed peas, as by January 1st, you can no longer source green pods. The black-eyed peas abundance is said to bring an abundance of good luck.

Serves 6

1 lb / 500 g dried black-eyed peas salt
⅓ cup lemon juice
½ cup olive oil
1 tbsp ground coriander seeds
⅓ tsp cumin
⅓ cup raw tahini
⅔ tbsp crushed garlic
⅔ tbsp dried mint leaves
⅔ tbsp fresh thyme

Rinse the black-eyed peas with plenty of water.
Place the black-eyed peas in a large pot with water to cover.
Bring the peas to a boil and cook on low heat for about an hour till the peas are tender.
Test by pressing 1 black-eyed pea, if it is easily mashed, remove from heat.
Transfer to a mixing bowl and add the rest of the ingredients.
Mix well.
Process in a food processor to a coarse paste.

Chickpea Salad

And Chickpeas for All

Chickpeas are one of eight Neolithic founder crops, domesticated by the farming communities in the Fertile Crescent about 10,000 years ago. They mark the agricultural revolution and the transition from nomadic hunters and gatherers to settlers.

Chickpeas are the basis for both hummus and falafel, food staples in the Middle East. Interestingly, these vegan dishes eaten together with a grain, like pita bread, produce a complete protein that may serve as a meat substitute for the meat-free.

In 2007, a team of Israeli scientists published their study of the origin of chickpeas and established that chickpeas were cultivated in the Middle East from a specific variation of a similar legume, found in Turkey. The cultivated variety was significantly richer in amino acids compared to the wild variety. As a result, when chickpeas are digested, high levels of serotonin, aka the happy chemical, are released. Their glorious contribution to nutrition and happiness, allowing the population to widen and become agriculture-based, feeding on crops instead of livestock, is still very much alive today. And the answer to the question *who ate hummus first?* seems to be older than the countries involved in the feud.

Serves 4

1¼ cup / 250 g dried chickpeas or 3 cups cooked or canned chickpeas

½ tbsp salt

1 tsp freshly ground black pepper

2 cloves garlic, crushed

2 tbsp lemon juice

½ cup /120 ml tahini sauce (page 225)

olive oil

1 tsp sumac

The night before, place the dried chickpeas in a bowl with cold water and soak overnight.

Drain, and place in a stock pot with water to cover by about 1 inch / 2 cm.

Bring to a boil and then cook over low heat for 2 hours, until the chickpeas are tender.

Drain the chickpeas and place in a large bowl. Spread the salt, black pepper, and garlic and lightly crush the chickpeas using a masher.

Mix together with the lemon juice. Divide the salad into four serving bowls.

Drizzle with tahini sauce and olive oil and sprinkle with the sumac.

Hummus

Serves 6

For the chickpeas:

1 cup / 200 g dried chickpeas

For the hummus:

3 cups / 600 g cooked chickpeas

1 tbsp chickpea cooking water

1-2 cloves garlic

1 tsp salt

⅛ tsp ground cumin

2 tbsp olive oil

2 tbsp lemon juice

¾ cup raw tahini

To make the chickpeas:

Soak the chickpeas overnight in plenty of water.

Drain and place in a large stockpot with plenty of water.

Cook for about 2 hours until the chickpeas are tender and can be easily mashed between two fingers.

Dried chickpeas will triple in size when soaked and cooked.

We usually process large amounts and freeze them in serving-size bags.

To make the hummus:

Place all the ingredients excluding the tahini in a food processor, and blend to a fine paste.

If the paste is too dry, add more of the chickpea cooking water. Add the tahini and blend to a smooth texture. Taste to adjust salt and lemon juice.

We love eating the hummus with a hot pepper sauce (page 222).

When chickpeas are digested, high levels of serotonin, aka the happy chemical, are released. Their glorious contribution to nutrition and happiness, allowing the population to widen and become agriculture based, feeding on crops instead of livestock, is still very much alive today.

לאקליפטוס
The Eucalyptus
Chef Moshe Basso

Mujadara

Meatless Thursday

In Iraq, the designated laundry day was Thursday. As a result, lunch that day was a meatless meal, traditionally made with lentils. They had the *kitchri*, a dish of rice cooked with red lentils, served with sunny-side-up eggs, which is easy and relatively quick to cook. In Israel, my mother started cooking mujadara with green lentils, which used essentially the same cooking method, and was based on the same combination of lentils and rice. The dish produces protein when digested. It is a set-in-stone kind of meal, and servings are distributed between the grandkids.

A few years ago, my mother started sprouting the lentils a few days ahead, a practice that increases nutritional value, and helps with digestion. Since then, Ronny picked up the practice, and came up with a side dish made of crispy sprouted lentils. Keep in mind when cooking this dish that sprouting is optional, but is worth the effort.

In our family, as usual, serving options vary – some keep it simple, serving the mujadara as is. Some add yogurt and mix. Some add yogurt and a simple salad of tomatoes and cucumbers.

Serves 6

1 tsp olive oil
1 onion, cut into rings
4 cloves garlic, finely chopped
½ tsp cumin
1 cups green lentils
1¾ cup water
½ tsp ground turmeric
1½ tsp salt
¼ tsp black pepper
1 cup rice
1 tbsp olive oil

Heat the olive oil in a medium stock pot and add the onion, sauté until light golden, then add the garlic and cumin. Remove almost all the onion, leaving about a tenth in the pot, set aside.

Place the lentils (for sprouted lentils see below) and water to the pot, and add the ground turmeric, salt, and black pepper.

Bring to a boil and add the rice. Cook with the lid on for about 15-20 minutes until the water is absorbed.

Leave covered for 30 minutes, and then add the olive oil and the onion, mixing well.

Serve with yogurt.

Sprouting the lentils (optional):

Place the lentils in a large bowl and cover with plenty of water, soak for 12 hours.

Drain the water and let the lentils sit for 3-4 days, occasionally turn the lentils over, until sprouts begin to form.

Risotto Carmel Freekeh

Risotto Carmel Freekeh

And if thou bring a meal-offering of first-fruits unto the LORD, thou shalt bring for the meal-offering of thy first-fruits corn in the ear parched with fire, even groats of the fresh ear. Leviticus 2:14.

Freekeh – smoked green wheat – was harvested when it was still green in the days of the Bible. It was then thrown to the fire. The straw and chaff would burn and only the kernel of wheat would remain. To extract the grain from the ear of wheat, they had a rubbing or threshing process, which gave the freekeh its name – in Arabic, it means rubbing the hands together.

Emmer wheat, considered the "Mother of Wheat," was discovered by Aaron Aaronsohn in Israel in 1906. The difference between the domesticated species of wheat and the wild wheat is that when the wild grains ripen, the seed head shatters and the seeds spread to the wind. For that reason, in the old days, the wheat needed to be harvested early while still green, which preserved it and, in turn, its nutritional value.

In biblical lore, Carmel freekeh is always identified with King David. When his great grandmother, Ruth, comes to Israel at the time of the harvest, she is given a piece of cake of the *kali* – another name for the freekeh wheat. When he is still a young boy, David is sent by his father to the front of the battle to give his brothers *kali*. When he's hiding from Saul in the village of Carmel, Abigail brings him *kali*.

Serves 6

2 tbsp olive oil

2 onions, finely chopped

2 cups almond milk (store bought or see recipe, page 222)

1 tsp salt

½ tsp pepper

1 tsp fresh thyme

½ cup diced white button mushrooms (¼×¼ inch / ½×½ cm)

2 cups smoked green wheat

2 cups vegetable stock (store bought or see recipe, page 224)

Pour the stock into a pot and bring it to a simmer over medium-high heat. Keep the stock at a simmer.

Heat a heavy-bottomed pot over medium heat. Add 2 tablespoons of olive oil and tip the pan to coat it with the oil of the pan.

Add the onions and cook, stirring frequently with a wooden spoon, until the onions have softened but not browned.

Add the fresh mushrooms and thyme, season with pepper, and stir fry until they give off their liquid and are tender.

Add the cooked green wheat and cook, stirring constantly to coat it with the olive oil, for about 5 minutes.

Ladle in about 1 cup of the stock and stir constantly, until the green wheat absorbs the stock.

Continue to add the stock in ½ cup increments, stirring constantly, and only adding more once the stock has been completely absorbed by the green wheat.

After about 7 minutes, ladle in about 1 cup of almond milk and add salt, stirring constantly. Add the remaining almond milk, cook until the green wheat absorbs the liquid.

Chiga – Vegan Kubbeh

The *cig* (*or chiga*) *kofte* is the Turkish name of the *kibbeh nayyeh,* a raw meat kubbeh. Its vegetarian version is what we served at the Oxford food symposium in 2018. The theme of the symposium was seeds and the keynote address was about the domestication of wheat. This recipe is all about seeds – as bulgur is essentially wheat seeds.

Bulgur is in fact one of the first foods humanity processed. The motives of the advancement were, as always, the preservation of food, that is, pushing back the expiration date, as well as the strengthening of the crop. In the case of wheat, the desire was also to keep insects away. The means to that end was a simple method of parboiling the wheat after the harvest, thus ridding the berries of insect eggs and possible mold infestation. That was followed by a drying process, using dry heat, essentially the sun, as the cooked wheat was spread on rooftops, and occasionally stirred as is homemade granola.

Although the meaning of *cig* is "raw" and is irrelevant in this version, as it does not contain raw meat, the *kofte* part is still relevant. *Kofte* means grind, pound or beat, and the bulgur processing is definitely all about that.

We have witnessed in the past decades the increased popularity of vegan dishes, and are proud to be considered vegan friendly. We challenge ourselves to produce vegan variations that in some cases, even to sworn carnivores, surpass the original dish.

Serves 6

2⅔ cups / 500 g bulgur
salt
freshly ground black pepper
½ tsp dried chile flakes, optional
1 tbsp olive oil
2 small onions, finely chopped
5 large tomatoes, finely chopped, divided into halves or thirds
7 tbsp / 100 g tomato paste
½ cup warm water
3½ oz /100 g green onions, thinly chopped
3 tbsp fresh mint, finely chopped
3 tbsp fresh parsley, finely chopped
baby arugula, for garnish

Mix together the bulgur and spices in a large mixing bowl.
In a frying pan, heat the olive oil over medium-high heat and brown the onions.
Add 2 of the tomatoes and stir fry for about 4 minutes.
Add the fried onions and tomatoes to the bulgur and mix well.
Blend the tomato paste with the warm water, and add to the bulgur mixture.
Knead the bulgur mixture and add lukewarm water as needed to achieve a mix that holds itself together.
Add the green onions, mint, parsley and the rest of the tomatoes.
Mix well and adjust seasoning. Let rest for about half an hour.
With wet hands, form palm sized patties and place on serving plates. Garnish with some baby arugula and serve.

Meat and Chicken

Chicken Makloubeh

My first introduction to makloubeh was at a staff meal cooked by Abu Abedalla, who was a veteran sous chef from the Palestinian village of Battir. Despite my familiarity with the local Arab cuisine, up until that meal, I hadn't had the chance to eat makloubeh. The dish is cooked sometimes during Ramadan, or when food is needed to feed a large group of people.

The makloubeh Abu Abedalla cooked was wonderful. I was immediately captivated by its fragrance and its comforting casserole flavors. But the appearance was lacking in style, as it was piled on a large tin. To make it to the restaurant menu, presentation was cardinal. My first sentiment was that I needed to find a way to make this dish more aesthetically appealing.

Yet, I felt that the family style denouement should be preserved.

That was the birth of the makloubeh ceremony – a large round stainless-steel tray was placed as a cover of the large makloubeh pot, and then turned upside down on a central presentation table. Upside down is actually the meaning of makloubeh, so it was perfectly fitting that the ceremony would include that dramatic touch.

As the years passed, we added the ceremonial countdown from seven to zero, to commemorate the walls of Jericho falling down after the Israelites marched around them for the seventh time on the seventh day. The whole crowd in the restaurant joins and gathers together around the makloubeh, eliminating the metaphoric walls between them.

The makloubeh manages to create its beautiful magic of bringing people together as in a traditional village – to be fed and comforted and to rejoice.

Serves 6

6 drumsticks and chicken thighs

3 medium potatoes, sliced

1 small head cauliflower, separated into florets

1 medium eggplant, quartered and cut into ½ inch / 1½ cm thick slices

3 medium onions, thinly sliced

1 large tomato, thinly sliced

2½ cups basmati rice, rinsed well with cold water

3 tbsp extra-virgin olive oil

6 threads saffron

1 tbsp turmeric

½ tsp dried thyme

2 tsp nutmeg

dash of paprika

freshly ground black pepper to taste

sea salt to taste

Place the chicken in a pot and add saffron, turmeric, thyme, nutmeg, and pepper to taste.

Cover with water and bring to a boil. Simmer for an hour, then remove the chicken and save the liquid.

Sauté the potatoes in 1 tablespoon of oil in a non-stick pan until lightly golden, but not cooked through. Set aside.

Sauté the cauliflower in remaining oil. Set aside.

In the same pan, sauté the eggplant until lightly browned.

In a large pot, spread tomato and onion along the bottom and arrange chicken over the onion layer.

Place the eggplant slices between the chicken pieces.

Distribute the cauliflower over the top, and then repeat with the potato slices. Spread the rice over the potatoes. Add broth to cover the rice by ½ inch / 1½ cm.

Place the pot, uncovered, over a medium flame and let the liquid simmer 15 minutes.

Then cover the pot, reduce heat and cook on low for 30 to 45 minutes. Add more liquid if needed to keep the mixture slightly moist, but be careful not to add so much that the rice becomes sticky or risotto-like.

Test for doneness by removing the cover and sniffing; when it has a burnt smell it's ready.

Take a round metal tray and place on top of the pot. Turn the pot carefully over onto the tray, patting the top to release the chicken. Remove the pot and use a large spoon to scrape the yummy burnt bits onto the platter.

Hamin Macaroni

Serves 6

vegetable oil for frying
4 potatoes, peeled and sliced into ½ inch / 1 cm slices
2 tsp olive oil
1 onion, coarsely chopped
10 drumsticks or chicken thighs, or a mix
1 tsp salt
freshly ground black pepper
¾ tsp ground turmeric
1 tsp sweet paprika
½ tsp sumac, optional
8 whole garlic cloves
1 lb / 500 g macaroni pasta
2 cups / 500 ml tomato sauce (page 33)

Heat enough oil in a medium saucepan to allow deep frying.
Fry the potatoes until golden. Remove and set aside.
Place a large stockpot on medium heat and add the olive oil.
When the oil has heated, add the onion and cook for 3 minutes, then add the drumsticks and chicken thighs and the salt, pepper, and spices.
Stir the chicken until it browns, about 10 minutes.
Add the garlic cloves toward the end of the browning.
Remove the chicken-onion-garlic combination and set aside.

Cook the macaroni in plenty of boiling water for 5 minutes. Drain.
Place a layer of potatoes in the stockpot, add a bit of olive oil if needed. Arrange the chicken nicely on top, and close with more potatoes. Mix the macaroni in the tomato sauce and add to the chicken and potatoes pot. Cook on low heat for at least an hour.
If you cook this dish overnight, add 1½ cups of water, and check the water level again before leaving it to over-night cook.
If cooked in the oven, set the temperature for 250°F / 120°C.

Asado Gyros

Serves 4

4 thin flatbreads, or fresh pitas

1 tbsp olive oil

1⅓ lb / 600 g carved asado meat, cut into bite-size chunks

1 tsp shawarma spice mix

½ tsp salt

For the almond tzatziki:

1 cup almond yogurt (page 222)

½ cucumber, shredded

½ tsp salt

2 cloves garlic, minced

1 tsp lemon juice

2 tsp olive oil

1 tsp fresh dill, chopped

For the fresh salad:

1½ oz / 40 g bunch fresh mint, finely chopped

1½ oz / 40 g bunch cilantro, finely chopped

1½ oz / 40 g bunch parsley, finely chopped

2 small radishes, thinly sliced

½ red onion, thinly sliced

1 tsp lemon juice

olive oil

salt

sumac

Heat the olive oil in a pan over medium-high heat and add the asado meat. Sprinkle with the shawarma spice mix and salt.
Stir fry for about 3-4 minutes.
Set aside.

To make the almond tzatziki:

Prepare the tzatziki by mixing all the ingredients in a medium mixing bowl.

To make the fresh salad:

Prepare the salad by mixing all the salad ingredients in a medium bowl. Season to taste.

To serve, place a flatbread on each plate and spread 1 tablespoon of the tzatziki on the flatbread. Arrange the asado mix on it.
Top with the fresh salad.

Smoked Chicken

So, heap on the wood and kindle the fire. Cook the meat well, mixing in the spices; and let the bones be charred. Ezekiel 24:10.

Fire and smoke are primal. Cooking on an open fire is a social feast that resonates in many cultures from the biblical era until today as a happy time, a gathering of family and close friends.

Smoke is not just a side effect of that open fire. It has become a desired flavor on its own. We brought in our smoker as part of the traditional carnivore evenings in the restaurant. This addition was the backdrop of the quest to come up with the perfect dishes with which to introduce this distinctive adored smoky scent. Michal came up with a simple yet addictive recipe.

The time spent in the smoker is crucial to the cooking formula. Our collective preference was for a rich smoky flavor and we arrived at forty-five minutes in the smoker. The smoker timing can be adjusted; the important point is to also adjust the oven time to make sure the chicken is cooked through.

Another important choice concerns the smoker's wood chips. These have a range of character and flavor, and we usually opt for the fruit variety, particularly apple and cherry. If you don't own a smoker, there is a simple solution of using a smoker box in a regular grill or oven. It is affordable and easy to cook with.

Serves 4

3⅓ lb / 1½ kg large chicken, divided into 8 parts, or use only bone-in chicken thighs

For the marinade:

1 cup silan (date molasses)

½ cup soy sauce

¼ cup apple cider vinegar

For serving:

2 green onions, sliced

2 tsp sesame

To prepare and smoke the chicken:

Place the chicken in a glass dish.

In a medium mixing bowl, mix all the marinade ingredients.

Pour the marinade over the chicken and coat the chicken with the mixture.

Place plastic wrap over the dish holding the chicken and refrigerate overnight.

After the chicken has marinated, remove the chicken from the marinade and transfer the marinade into a medium saucepan.

Turn on the smoker and let it preheat to 225°F / 100°C.

If you don't own a smoker, an alternative is to use a smoker-box in a preheated oven or in a grill.

Smoke the chicken for about 45 minutes.

To make the glaze:

While the chicken is in the smoker, place the marinade saucepan over medium heat and bring to a simmer. Continue to cook over low heat, until the marinade is reduced, about 20 minutes.

To oven-cook the chicken:

Preheat the oven to 400°F / 200°C.

Remove the chicken from the smoker and brush it with the glaze.

Place the chicken on the oven's middle rack and cook for about an hour.

Heat a small pan over medium-high heat. Add the sesame and toast for about 4 minutes, stirring continually.

When ready to serve, divide the chicken and sprinkle it with the sliced green onions and the toasted sesame.

Aruk

Mining for Gold in Your Own Kitchen

There is a funny saying, *you can't make everyone happy, you're not pizza*, which touches the cornerstone of making food. This is true of your own family members, let alone the masses: you can almost never please everyone with one dish. My mother complains until this day of how my younger brother, who is 66 years old, ruined our breakfast routine 60 years ago, by announcing he will not eat sunny-side-up eggs for breakfast, thus causing a rebellion that both my sister and I joined. My mother needed to find alternatives for her spoiled kids.

Every home cook struggles with the crowd pleaser. After the egg fiasco, my mother found an exception to the "you can't please everyone rule" with a gem of

a dish: aruk. These patties please the most difficult eaters in the family.

These are not served freely. Whenever my mother makes them, she automatically rations the specific number of patties one may have.

If you happen to walk in on her when she is frying them, she keeps an eye on you when you near the succulent batch cooling on a rack, like a veteran hawk. Likewise, these are not left on the stove for any starved grandkid to walk in, lift the lid, and make a quick food-grab. Were it otherwise, the patties would be consumed within minutes. After they are meticulously allocated, the rations are hidden in the back of the fridge, saved for the lucky ones.

My daughter, Sharon, learned how to cook them, then told me she felt like she had struck gold. As an added plus, you can serve them the next day, cold or reheated, and no one complains.

There is a bit of a hassle in manually cutting the chicken breast into diced pieces, but it's totally worth the work. The diced pieces keep the chicken tender and succulent. It is important to mention that my daughter recently adapted this recipe to hectic modern-day life by blitzing the chicken breast in a food processor. She reports great success with keeping the texture and saving time.

Another important note concerns the baharat spice mix used in this recipe. The seasoning is comprised of salt and baharat. That specific blend is Iraqi baharat, the one used for *tbit*. It can be easily ground in-house then kept in the freezer for future use.

Ronny likes to stuff the aruk into a bun with some mayo, thin slices of tomato, and arugula, which turns into an energizing grab-on-the-go.

Makes about 40 patties

2 lb / 1 kg chicken breast

1 big onion, thinly chopped

5 oz / 140 g flat leaf parsley, thinly chopped stalks included

2 large zucchinis, coarsely grated

2 carrots, grated

1 heaping tsp Iraqi tbit baharat (store bought or see recipe, page 233)

2 tsp salt

3 eggs

1 cup whole grain spelt flour or all-purpose flour

sunflower oil for frying

There are two ways to prepare the chicken breast:

Place the chicken breast in a food-processor and blitz until it is minced.

Or, dice the chicken breast into ¼ inch / 1 cm pieces.

Place into a large mixing bowl.

Add the chopped onion and parsley. Blend in the zucchini and carrots.

Add the spices and mix well. Add the eggs and flour, combining into a uniform mixture.

Pour the oil into a large frying pan, so that there is a layer of oil about $^{1}/_{14}$ inch / 2 mm, or even less for a good non-stick pan.

Heat the pan over medium-high heat.

Scoop a spoonful of the mixture and drop it into the pan.

Flatten it a bit if needed.

Fry for about 2-3 minutes on each side, turning when golden, and repeat with the rest of the mixture.

Jerusalem Mixed Grill

If you happen to be walking down Agripas Street in the evening or nighttime, coming from the Machane Yehuda Market to the west, you will find yourself immersed in the mixed grill scents flooding out of the restaurants, drifting uphill on the western wind, rolling through the city center, over the walls and in through the gates of the Old City, and from there, making a right angle up to heaven. These diet breaking fragrances, even when I'm full, will always make me run – as a hungry man runs to the doors of a bakery when bread is baking – to the window of Micha's and Avi's Hazot restaurant.

The same smells swept Jerusalem in the ancient days of pilgrimage, when the city was a festival of grilled meats of lamb, calves, pigeons, and goats. The burnt offering meats were eaten wrapped in a thin flatbread, which today is called Iraqi pita or laffa.

Jerusalem, when the Temples stood, was a prominent culinary center. Along with the burnt offerings, there were first fruit offerings, and offerings of olive oil, semolina, and wine. In short, Jerusalem boasted a three-pilgrimage food and wine festival according to the law of Moses and Israel.

Legend has it, on one stormy winter's night at the end of 1969, high winds had blown out the fire in the Hazot restaurant's charcoal grill and had caused the clientele to flee. As the owners started planning their own homeward escape, a VIP client arrived, and asked to be fed.

There were all kinds of skewered meats standing by, but no fire in the grill. Such an important diner was not to be let down. But how do you quickly make him happy with a cold grill? As it happened, on the small gas stove that was generally used to make

Turkish coffee, there stood a square metal cover. This could be used as a food grill, they realized, and the first Jerusalem mixed grill was born. Onions were seared on the hot metal cover, and the meats were un-skewered and seared on the metal plate with fresh seasoning and a dollop of amba. Micha tasted the mix and a smile spread across his face, as he rolled his new discovery in Iraqi flatbread.

Over time, the entire Agripas street has turned into a street of secret labs and test kitchens that create new seasonings and strive to reach new culinary peaks.

Serves 4

For the mixed grill:

sunflower oil

3 onions, coarsely chopped

100 g entrecote, cut into ¾ inch×3 inch / 2 cm×8 cm strips

100 g turkey, cut into ¾ inch×3 inch / 2 cm×8 cm strips

100 g chicken breast, cut into ¾ inch×3 inch / 2 cm×8 cm strips

100 g chicken liver, each cut in half

100 g chicken spleen

For the spice mix:

1 tbsp ground turmeric

1 tbsp curry

1 tsp ground nutmeg

1 tsp sweet paprika

1 tsp pungent paprika

1 tsp freshly ground coriander seeds

½ tsp ground white pepper

½ tsp freshly ground black pepper

½ tsp freshly ground allspice

½ tsp salt

Place the spices in a small bowl and mix well.

Place the meats in a bowl and make sure they are blended together. Add 1 tablespoon of the spice mix to the meat bowl and mix.

In a large non-stick wok or skillet, heat oil and add the onions, stir fry for 2 minutes.

Add a tablespoon of the spice mix, while stirring the onions and spices.

Add the meat and continue to stir, add 2 tablespoons of oil, and about half a spoon of the spices.

Stir fry for about 6-7 minutes.

Tokyo-Jerusalem Gyoza

Ronny likes to explore the world. For him, much of the merit of any travel destination is the local cuisine. He immediately translates that special interest into new imagined combinations for his favorite at-home dishes. On his return, we have learned to expect his clever pairings and innovations.

Ronny said an idea came to him while eating gyoza dumplings in Tokyo. He then-and-there decided to make a Tokyo-Jerusalem mix. Lamb sprang to his mind as it is so intrinsic to the Israeli food scene. When he returned from that illuminating visit to Japan, he introduced the new dish at the New Year table. It was made of gyoza dumplings filled with succulent lamb with an herbal surprise, all in a savory sauce. That dish was hailed and devoured accordingly.

The idea of marrying zhoug and soy to create the sauce brings a synergy of flavors: the zhoug tones down the salty soy and enhances the flavors of the lamb and mint.

Makes 30 gyoza dumplings

1 package gyoza wrappers (30 units)

For the gyoza mix:

½ oz / 15 g parsley, finely chopped

½ oz / 15 g mint, finely chopped

1 scant tsp thyme, finely chopped

1⅕ oz / 35 g green onion, thinly sliced

5⅓ oz / 150 g white cabbage, finely chopped

1 lb / 450 g mix of ground lamb and beef

3½ oz / 100 g white button mushrooms, finely chopped

1 tsp salt

¼ tsp freshly ground black pepper

vegetable oil for frying

water

For the dipping sauce:

2 tbsp soy sauce

2 tbsp freshly squeezed lime juice

2 heaping tbsp zhoug (store bought or see recipe, page 222)

1 tsp chile oil

To make the gyoza:

Combine the ingredients in a medium mixing bowl, mix well, and knead with your hands.

Keep the wrappers under a damp towel while preparing the gyoza, to prevent them from drying out.

Place a wrapper in the palm of your hand and pile a teaspoon of filling onto the center of the wrapper.

Fold the wrapper in half over the filling, start making pleats every ¼ inch / ½ cm from the center moving to the right edge. Then repeat from the center to the left edge.

Heat about 1 tablespoon of oil in a large non-stick frying pan over medium heat. When the pan is hot, place the gyoza in a single layer, flat side down in a circular pattern, making sure to not overcrowd the pan.

Cook for about 3 minutes, until the bottom of the gyoza turns golden.

Add about ¼ cup of water to the pan and cover immediately.

Cook for 3 minutes.

Transfer to a plate and serve with the dipping sauce.

Drizzle some drops of chile oil onto the serving plate.

To make the dipping sauce:

Combine the soy sauce, lime, and zhoug in a small mixing bowl. Mix together. Taste and adjust.

Kubbeh Patata

Raisin Wars

The most beloved holiday dish of our family is without a doubt a type of kubbeh (stuffed dumpling) which ascends to our table only once in a blue moon, or, more literally, only on a full or new moon. This dish is only prepared on two of the three Pilgrimage Festivals, Sukkot and Passover – both are always celebrated when the moon is full – and on the Jewish New Year, when the moon is new.

These crunchy patties are fought over, and even when 70 pieces are made for 20 eager, normally loving, family members, it gets ugly. Families (without mentioning names) are torn over their raisin preferences, and one cannot easily decide if he likes better the brother who loves raisins, and who is therefore not in competition over the patties, or the cousin who is a comrade in the anti-raisins regiment, hence coveting the same beloved patties.

Nor is it an easy task to prepare this kubbeh, as is becoming for a dish worthy of such eminent status. The chicken breast is meticulously cut into cubes using a sharp knife, the onions are evenly chopped. The golden seared onion-chicken breast mix is delicately wrapped in the potato puree balls. Then comes the careful batch frying, making sure not to bruise the patties when turning them over. No one ever manages to do a decent job in the scrutinizing eyes of my mother. She is right of course, hers are the only ones not bursting from too much filling and that come out of the frying pan with an even golden tan and a fresh crunch.

Raisins are adored by some, optional for those who are downright opportunistic, and loathed by the most bratty among the grandkids and great-grandkids of my mother.

Makes about 35 kubbeh

4½ lb / 2 kg Yukon gold potatoes, peeled
1¾ lb / 800 g chicken breast diced about ¼ by ¼ inch / ½ by ½ cm
3 medium onions, finely chopped
3½ oz / 100 g raisins, optional
1 tsp salt
½ tsp black pepper, freshly ground
1½ tsp Iraqi *tbit* baharat spice mix (store bought or see recipe, page 233)
1 tsp salt
3-4 tbsp potato flour
2 tbsp olive oil
sunflower oil for frying
1 egg white, beaten

Boil the potatoes in a pot with lots of water. Cook until a fork easily slides in.

Drain and immediately mash to a finely textured puree. You can use a ricer or a food mill, if you have them, though a potato masher is sufficient for the desired texture. Allow the puree to completely chill.

Add salt and potato flour to the mashed potatoes and knead to a smooth paste. Divide the mixture into ping-pong-sized balls. Set aside.

Heat the olive oil in a large sauté pan over medium-low heat, add the onion and cook for about 5 minutes until translucent. Add the cubed chicken and spices. Stir until the chicken turns white. Taste and add more salt if needed. Remove from heat and allow to cool. Add the raisins and mix well.

Flatten a potato ball using your hands and fill with about a teaspoon of the seared chicken and onions mixture. Close the ball, folding tightly. Flatten the kubbeh and apply the egg wash before you fry it.

Pour enough oil into a frying pan to come 1¼ inch / 3 cm up the sides. Place over medium heat and wait until the oil is hot. Fry the kubbeh for about 2-3 minutes on each side until golden. Place the kubbeh on a plate lined with a paper towel to soak up excess oil.

Lamb with Artichoke and Green Almonds

The green almonds may be replaced with fava beans.

Serves 4

1 tbsp olive oil
1 onion, coarsely chopped
1½ lb / 700 g boneless lamb shoulder
1 tsp salt
½ tbsp ground black pepper
1 tsp ground allspice
½ tsp sumac
4 sprigs fresh thyme, or 1 tsp dried leaves
5 large artichokes, cleaned and cut into eighths, in lemon water
1 lb / 500 g green almonds
1 tbsp olive oil
lemon juice from 1 lemon

Heat the olive oil in a large dutch oven, over medium-high heat.

Add the chopped onion and the lamb cuts and evenly brown, adding salt, black pepper, allspice, sumac, and 3 sprigs of fresh thyme, stirring occasionally.
When all the meat is browned all over, add water to cover and cook on low heat for 45 minutes.
Drain the artichokes.

Heat a sauté pan over medium heat, and add the artichokes and green almonds, stir once.
Add 2 tablespoons of olive oil and stir fry for several minutes, adding ¼ tsp black pepper and 1 sprig of fresh thyme. Add the lemon juice and a cup of the lamb cooking fluids, cook for 7 minutes.
When the lamb has cooked through, add the artichokes and almonds with the broth to the lamb pot and cook for 15 minutes more.

This dish is best served with white rice.

Ingria – Sweet and Sour Beef and Eggplant Stew

Follow the Spice Trail

Uncovering a pot and breathing in the scented steam takes me on a journey back to the origins of those spices.

I remember from my childhood, the aroma of my mother's and grandmother's cooking. Back then in Jerusalem, post Israel's declaration of independence, we didn't have restaurants, or new cuisines. Basically, people ate home-cooked meals and couldn't really afford anything else. Consequently, only when I grew up and had eaten outside of my close-knit family circle, did I realize that even the specific dishes I had known all my life had different interpretations in different homes.

This recipe of *ingria* was a common dish in my mother's kitchen. It is an eggplant and beef stew, with a sauce that my mother made with tomatoes, lemon, and sugar.

I thought that was it, that was *ingria*. And then I learned that other Iraqi Jews cooked it in different ways. Some would replace the beef strips with beef cutlets; this variation was created in Israel, because in Iraq, when they say meat, they mean lamb, exclusively. Some would add tamarind to the sauce.

I was very fond of the tamarind version, and I wondered about the origin of the tamarind in the sauce. With time, I learned there had been a community of Jewish Iraqi textile merchants, who were living between India and Iraq, spending several years here and then there.

These trade routes saw the adoption of new habits, and cooking styles were among them. They brought

with them amba – a condiment made from pickled ripe mango with curry, which upgraded the sabich – the Saturday morning eggplant and eggs sandwich – to a stellar status, and the tamarind fruit, which the local Iraqi community embraced and started to cook with.

My mother still remembers how they cooked using a primus stove to sear the onions and lamb chunks, and how they then set the pot on a kerosene burner where it spent time on the actual, non-metaphorical, backburner. To this day, in my mother's *ingria* recipe, you will find the sweet and sour of the tomato-sugar-lemon alone, but to the best of my knowledge, she doesn't frown on my addition of the tangy tamarind.

Serves 6

2 tbsp olive oil
2 medium onions, sliced into a ¼ inch / ½ cm rings
1½ lb / 700 g beef chuck, cut into ½ inch / 1½ cm slices
1 tsp freshly ground black pepper
2 tsp ground allspice
¾ tsp salt
3 sprigs fresh or dry thyme
1 onion, diced coarsely
2 cups vegetable stock or boiling water
2 large eggplants, light and shiny, sliced into ⅓ inch / 1 cm round slices
vegetable oil
2 quinces or Granny Smith apples, cut into ¼ inch / ½ cm round slices
3-4 medium tomatoes, cut into ¼ inch / ½ cm slices
1 cup crushed tomatoes
4 tbsp tamarind paste
3-4 tbsp silan, date molasses, can be replaced by maple syrup

Preheat the oven to 400°F / 200°C.
Heat the olive oil in a heavy-bottomed pot on medium-high heat, add the onion rings and cook until golden, about 5-7 minutes.

Remove the onions from the pot, trying to keep the rings intact.
Place the beef strips in the pot, and add the salt, black pepper, allspice, thyme, and diced onion.
Stir until the onions are golden and the beef is seared on all sides, add the stock and lower the heat.
Cover and let simmer for an 1½ hours until the beef is tender. If needed, add more water or stock.
Add the crushed tomatoes, tamarind paste, and silan to the pot and bring to a boil, dissolving the tamarind paste.
Remove from heat.

While the beef is cooking, place the eggplant slices on a sheet and lightly brush vegetable oil on both sides.
Place on a rack in a single layer and roast for 10 to 15 minutes. Flip the eggplant slices halfway through for even browning.

Add a ladleful of the beef cooking broth to a casserole dish, and evenly layer the eggplant. Place the beef strips on the eggplant, and layer the apples or quince on top. Place a second layer of the eggplant, set the golden onions in a single layer, and top with a layer of tomato slices. Add more broth, but just to cover the beef.
Bake for 30 minutes. Serve with white rice.

Pastilla – Duck Confit

In 2002, we held Eucalyptus's first halachic dinner, that is, a feast of forgotten kosher birds and animals, which serves as a means to preserve and pass on culinary traditions. Halacha is the collective body of Jewish religious laws based on the written biblical descriptions and oral traditions. Interestingly, the slaughter of sheep and cattle is stated to be, *as I have commanded you*, Deuteronomy 12:22; however, in the five books of Moses, the instructions are nowhere to be found. Part of halacha is the codifying of ritual slaughter laws that were passed on from generation to generation, but which have now been largely forgotten by the general public, as most of us purchase our meat from the supermarket. The main idea of the halachic dinner was to present different kosher species as a vehicle to preserve these ancient, forgotten, kosher traditions.

One of the eighteen species that we served was pheasant, and we were given just 10 skinny pheasants to feed 250 diners. To make things more challenging, we were required to prepare the pheasant in such a way that diners were able to hold a piece with their fingers for the traditional blessing – and the idea for pheasant pastillas was born.

In order to enrich the flavor of the pheasant and to ensure the 10 birds would be enough for everyone, we added dried fruit and caramelized onions and encased the mixture in filo pastry. The resulting special pastilla is still served daily, with the pheasant substituted with duck, a more common species but equally delicious.

Makes about 36 pastillas

1 tbsp coarse sea salt

1 tsp nutmeg, freshly ground

2 tsp freshly ground allspice

2 tsp ground cinnamon

1 tbsp ground coriander seeds

½ tsp ground cardamom

¼ tsp hot paprika

½ tsp freshly ground black pepper
3⅓ lb / 1.5 kg whole duck
2 medium onions, coarsely chopped
12 prunes, pitted
6 dried figs
36 circles of *feuilles de brick* pastry 9 inch / 22 cm in diameter – can be substituted with spring-roll wrappers or filo pastry
2 tbsp white flour
water
sunflower oil, for frying

Preheat the oven to 425°F / 220°C. Mix together all the spices for a spice rub and set aside a quarter of the spice-rub mix. Rub the mixture all over the duck inside and out. Place the duck straight onto the bars of the middle shelf of the oven. Place 1 of the chopped onions in the bottom of a large, deep-sided roasting tray. Place this tray on the bottom shelf beneath the duck. It should catch the fat that drips out of the duck.
Roast for 30 minutes and then lower the temperature to 300°F / 150°C.
Move the duck to the roasting tray and roast for another 90 minutes, until the duck is tender and can be easily pulled from the bone.
Let cool and cut into 1 inch / 2.5 cm by ¼ inch / 0.5 cm strips.
Spoon about 2 tbsp of the fat into a saucepan and place on medium heat. Add the remaining chopped onion and cook for about 8 minutes until golden. Remove from heat.
Chop the dried fruit into ¼×¼ inch / ½×½ cm cubes.
Place the duck in a bowl and add the onion and the dried fruit, mix together with the remaining spice mix.

Mix the flour with a little water to form a sticky dough.
Place 1 pastry circle on a clean surface and spread about 2 tablespoons of the duck mixture in a thin strip of 4¾ inch×1 inch / 12 cm×2 cm on the edge closest to you, leaving 1 inch / 2.5 cm clear from the edge.
Fold the two sides over the mixture to hold it in and roll away from you to create a cigar. Seal the top with a little bit of the sticky dough.

Pour enough oil into a frying pan to come 1¼ inch / 3 cm up the sides. Place over medium heat and wait until the oil is hot. Fry the pastilla for about 2-3
minutes until golden. Place the pastilla on a plate lined with a paper towel to soak up excess oil.

For the carrot cream:
4 carrots, about 14 oz / 400 g
2 cups water
½ cup sugar
½ tsp pure vanilla extract
½ cup turmeric oil (store bought or see recipe, page 227)

To make the carrot cream:
Peel and trim the carrots and place in a medium saucepan, add the water. Bring to a boil and then simmer for about 20 minutes until the carrots are soft, and a fork slides in easily. Reserve ½ cup of the carrots' cooking water.
Put the cooked carrots in a food processor and start processing, gradually pouring in the carrot water. Add the sugar and vanilla and continue to process to a smooth creamy consistency.
Add the turmeric oil and blend to create an emulsion.

For the red wine sauce:
1½ cup / 375 ml red wine
½ cup / 100 g sugar

To make the red wine sauce:
Combine the wine and sugar in a small saucepan and simmer over low heat for about 30 minutes to reduce.

To serve:
Halve the duck pastilla diagonally. Place two spoonfuls of carrot cream on separate sides of a flat serving dish, use the back of a ladle to spread the cream in a circular motion. Place the pastilla cigars within the inner circle and drizzle the wine reduction on top.

Mulard in Spices and Braised Jerusalem Artichoke

We like to serve it with risotto freekeh (see recipe, page 112)

Serves 6

3 mulard breasts or other large duck breasts, skin on

For the spice infusion:

1½ tsp cinnamon
3 tbsp fresh chopped thyme
1½ tsp sugar
3 tbsp ground coriander seeds
6 fresh dates, halved and stoned
14 oz / 400 g green beans
18 cherry tomatoes on the vine

For the Jerusalem artichoke:

Olive oil
1 large onion, thinly sliced
1 lb / 500 g Jerusalem artichoke, peeled
4 cups / 1 liter vegetable stock or water
pinch of saffron or 1 tsp turmeric
1 tsp salt
½ tsp freshly ground black pepper

To make the infusion:

If the layer of fat on the mulard is very thick, slightly trim it. Place the cinnamon, sugar, coriander, and half the thyme into a small mixing bowl and mix. Massage the spice mix onto both sides of the breasts and let it sit at room temperature to infuse the duck with the flavors. In the meantime, prepare the Jerusalem artichoke and the freekeh risotto.

To prepare the braised Jerusalem artichoke:

In a heavy bottomed pot that can go into the oven, heat olive oil to coat the bottom of the pan. Sauté the onion until golden, about 5 minutes.

Add the Jerusalem artichoke and brown on all sides.

Add enough vegetable stock to almost cover the artichokes, bring to a boil, and add the saffron or turmeric and the salt and pepper.

Place a tight-fitting lid and reduce the heat. simmer for at least 30 minutes without opening the lid. Then check with a fork if they are tender.

If they are still too firm, cover again and cook for 15 minutes longer.

To make the mulard:

Bring a medium pot of water to boil and add 1 tablespoon of salt. Place the green beans into the boiling water and cook for 3 minutes. drain the green beans and set aside.

Preheat the oven to 400°F / 200 °C.

Heat a grill pan on high heat, and place the mulard, skin side down on the pan, add the dates to the pan, cut side down to soften. Add the cherry tomatoes as well, to blister the skin and soften. Flip the mulard breast after seven minutes and cook for four more minutes on the meat side.

Remove from the pan, sprinkle the rest of the thyme and finish in the oven until it is cooked medium, about 5-10 minutes. Let the duck, dates, and tomatoes rest for a couple of minutes out of the oven.

Add the green beans to the hot pan to heat through.

To serve, place a heap of the freekeh, add the Jerusalem artichoke, slice the breast in half and stack onto the artichoke, garnish with the green beans, tomatoes, and dates.

Liver Pate Macarons

Sharbel Ishaq, our beloved customer service manager, has been with us for eight years. He started as a waiter, and elegantly worked his way up. Sharbel grew up in the Armenian Quarter of the Old City, a few minutes' walk from the restaurant, and still resides there. When he was an apprentice waiter, he came up with the idea to serve macaron cookies with liver pate filling.

This combination of the sweet and savory is contrasted with the raspberries coulis. When we first tested the accompanying liver pate, I used the recipe of my Hungarian Jewish mother-in-law, Naomi, for the chopped liver. In Hungary, the essential ingredient is schmaltz, poultry fat, because kosher laws prohibit the use of butter. In the restaurant, we are lucky to have our own source of schmaltz, as a byproduct of roasted duck for the pastillas.

Kosher laws also refer to the cooking of chicken liver. In the case of liver, salting to draw out the blood is not sufficient. It calls for a special broiling process. I find grilling or broiling help to avoid metallic tastes that often develop in liver. If you have the option to use an open fire such as a broiler or charcoal grill, it contributes great caramelized flavor.

Makes 24 macarons

For the liver filling:

2½ tbsp goose fat (or olive oil)

2-3 onions, coarsely chopped (10 oz / 300 g in total)

13 oz / 375 g chicken liver, cleaned

½ tsp salt

½ tsp freshly ground black pepper

1 tbsp brandy or whiskey

24 macaron cookies

For the raspberry coulis:

7 oz / 200 g raspberries or mixed berries

3 tbsp sugar

To make the liver filling:

Heat the goose fat in a large heavy skillet over medium-high heat.

Once hot, add the onions and stir about 7 minutes. Reduce the heat and cook until soft and golden.

Preheat the oven to 460°F / 240°C and spread the chicken livers on a baking pan set with parchment paper. Broil for about 2-3 minutes on each side.

Place the chicken livers on the onions and add the salt and pepper, cook on high heat for 3 minutes, stirring continually. Add the brandy and tilt the skillet to ignite the vapors, or stir for about 2 minutes, either way, the alcohol will vaporize.

Remove from heat and allow to cool for about 10 minutes.

Place in a food processor and process till smooth, but not too fine.

Place the macarons upside down on a plate. Transfer the liver pate to a pastry bag, and pipe, using a star icing tip, about 1 oz / 30 g liver pate onto each macaron.

To make the raspberry coulis:

Place the berries and sugar in a small saucepan on low heat. Simmer for about 7 minutes and process in a food processor till smooth.

Sugar amount should be adjusted to the sourness of the berries. The desired flavor should be mildly sour, not sweet.

To serve:

Brush a plate with raspberry coulis and gently place a macaron on top, add a drizzle of coulis on top of each macaron. Decorate with small edible flowers.

Fish

Fish Siniyah

Serves 6

sunflower oil, for frying

1½ lb / 700 g potatoes, peeled and cut into ¼ inch / ½ cm slices

6 grey mullet fillets (about 4¼ oz / 120 g fillet), skinned and pin bones removed

olive oil

salt

freshly ground black pepper

freshly ground allspice

For the sauce:

10 oz / 300 g tahini paste

1 cup water

⅓ cup freshly squeezed lemon juice

1-2 cloves garlic, crushed

salt

Pour the sunflower oil into a medium saucepan to a depth of about 1 ½ inch / 3 cm and place over medium-high heat.

Place the potatoes in the hot oil and fry for about 4 minutes until golden.

Rub the fish fillets with olive oil, salt, black pepper, and allspice.

Preheat the oven to 425°F / 220°C.

Cook the sauce by placing the tahini paste, water, and lemon juice in a small saucepan over medium heat. Gently whisk to blend the mixture. Add the garlic. Bring to a mild boil while whisking.

Arrange the potatoes in a single layer on a baking dish (ceramic or metal preferred).

Place the fillets on top.

Pour the warm tahini sauce on the fish to cover, plus a little surplus and bake for about 20 minutes.

Siniyah encourages family style meals, which we love – sitting together with companions, eating and spending time together.

In this recipe, we celebrate the reunion of tahini with fish, complementing each other beautifully.

Grilled Grey Mullet with Cilantro Pesto

Incense Offerings

Whenever I'm making pesto, my heart fills with song. The mortar and pestle were among the tools of the altar of incense. Eventually they were plundered by Titus, and so are depicted on the Arch of Titus in Rome alongside the menorah and silver trumpets.

It is said that sins were to be forgiven by the burnt offerings and that the smoke of the incense was to signify an offered prayer. The sacred incense was burnt at the Temple every morning and every evening. The prayer that now replaces the burning of the incense commemorates its components and includes the words the High Priest would say as he ground the incense with mortar and pestle: *Press well, well press, because the sound is good for the spices.* Pitum ha-Ketoret prayer.

However, we find the mortar and pestle mentioned long before the building of the Temples. They were carried through the desert, this time as kitchen tools, and not as sacred Temple relics. The mere mention of those tools in the middle of the desert, proves their indispensability. These were people fleeing their homes by God's command with only their unrisen bread. Yet here they are, with the tool needed to ground the manna. The manna is mentioned with coriander, one of the few times coriander is referred to in the Bible.

Now the manna resembled coriander seed, and its appearance was like that of gum resin. The people walked around and gathered it, ground it on a hand mill or crushed it in a mortar, then boiled it in a cooking pot or shaped it into cakes. It tasted like pastry baked with fine oil. Numbers 11: 7–8.

In our recipe, as manna can't be sourced regularly, we'll use coriander and add oil and walnuts. Also, the food processor replaces the glorified mortar and pestle, though those tools can indeed still be used. If you wish to use a mortar and pestle, please raise your voice in song, as the sound is good for the spices.

Serves 6

1½ cup / 75 g cilantro

3 cloves garlic

½ cup / 80 g toasted walnuts

1 tsp ground coriander seeds (optional)

¾ tsp salt

3 tbsp olive oil

3 tbsp lemon juice

2¼ lb / 1 kg grey mullet fillets, pin bones removed

Preheat the oven to 450°F / 230°C. Place the cilantro, garlic, walnuts, and coriander seeds in a food processor bowl, and pulse once. Add the salt and start processing as you drizzle the olive oil and lemon juice.

Place the fillets on a baking tray lined with parchment paper and massage the cilantro pesto onto the fillets. Grill for about 12 minutes until the fish is just cooked through.

Saint Peter's Fish

It would be an understatement to say there is a lot of interest in the world regarding Israel. Much of the hype around the restaurant and my own personal interest in cooking this specific cuisine are connected to the area – historically, biblically, and agriculturally. The hidden threads of the past, of the earth, and of the sun are intertwined in the innovation and tradition of the vibrant Israeli cuisine. For me, cooking and sharing this food is a way to preserve the past, to tell its stories through flavors and scents.

We have many groups of travelers coming to the restaurant to experience Israel's local plant- and herb-based cuisine. There is great interest in the Bible as a source of information conveying what it was like to live in Israel and Judea, all those years ago.

When I named our grilled tilapia dish, Saint Peter's fish, I was referring to the story of the apostle Peter who Jesus sent to catch a fish that was predicted to carry a coin in its mouth, by which Jesus and Peter would pay the tax of the land. Matthew 17:24-27.

Before Saint Peter became a saint or was called Peter the Apostle, he was called Simeon – or in the Greek form, Simon – and he was a Jewish fisherman living in the north of Israel. After witnessing the miracle in which Jesus healed Simeon's mother-in-law, and after the miraculous catch of fish, Peter joined Jesus. Peter ultimately became the first bishop of Rome and the first pope

And I tell you, you are Peter, and on this rock I will build my church, and the gates of hell shall not prevail against it. I will give you the keys of the kingdom of heaven, and whatever you bind on earth shall be bound in heaven, and whatever you loose on earth shall be loosed in heaven. Matthew 16:18-19.

Peter's story tells the primal story of Christianity, not at all well known to people following the Jewish faith. Nevertheless, it is an important link between the faiths, and in my opinion, shows a connection between the people who follow the Old Testament and those who follow the New Testament. As the stories of Simon/Peter are only told in the New Testament and not in the Old Testament, this could be a bond that may strengthen the connection between the faiths and yet allow each faith its individuality.

I am grateful to be living in times in which many people look for unity and ways to establish relations between cultures and faiths, rather than for ways to separate themselves. I am grateful to have the opportunity to have beautiful conversations with travelers coming to dine at The Eucalyptus, to enable them to experience a place of tolerance and coexistence, and to tell my story. In a way, this is my humble mission, to bring people together unified by love of food.

Serves 4

4 garlic cloves, crushed
2 tbsp cilantro, coarsely chopped
2 tsp sumac
1 tsp sea salt
2 tbsp olive oil
2 whole tilapia (St. Peter's Fish) (about 3½ lb / 1½ kg in total), cleaned, heads and tails left intact

For the dipping sauce:

2 garlic cloves, crushed
2 tbsp freshly squeezed lemon juice
4 tbsp soy sauce
2 tbsp cilantro, coarsely chopped
⅓ chile pepper, finely sliced, optional
1 small dried lime (Persian lime or *noomi basra*), seeds removed and crushed

Prepare a medium-high 400°F/ 200°C gas or charcoal grill fire. Brush the grill grates with oil several times to ensure a nonstick surface.

Place the garlic, cilantro, sumac, sea salt, and 1 tablespoon of the olive oil in a small mixing bowl and mix well.

Using a sharp knife, make 2 long, ¼ inch / ½ cm deep diagonal slashes 2 inch / 5 cm apart on both sides of the fish.

Rub the spice mix inside the fish, working it all into the slashes.

Rub both sides of each fish with the remaining olive oil.

Place the fish on the grill. Cook for about 5 to 7 minutes, until the flesh along the undersides turns opaque.

Place the dipping sauce ingredients in a medium mixing bowl and mix thoroughly.

Oriental Ceviche

When Ronny travelled to Peru, he pretty quickly found himself working in the prestigious Gaston Acurio restaurants – the Astrid Y Gaston and La Mar Cebicheria kitchens. It was an immensely educating experience where he picked up Peruvian techniques. The traditional Peruvian cooking method for ceviche relies mainly on citric acid, most commonly lime juice, to cook the fish. There is a delicate point of balance in which the fish is no longer raw, and yet the citric juice has not gone all the way through to create a crumbly texture. The ideal texture timetable puts the preferred timing between 5 and 20 minutes from the time the lime juice is added.

Our ceviche adds a layer of olive oil, coating the fish and keeping its texture firm.

The kohlrabi was an added inheritance from the vegan version. We found it complements the dish and adds balance.

The fish for the dish should be the absolute freshest available.

Serves 6 as a starter

14 oz / 400 g yellowtail amberjack, Spanish mackerel, or drum fillet, skinned and pin bones removed
2½ tbsp olive oil
4 tbsp cilantro, chopped
7 oz / 200 g kohlrabi
7 oz / 200 g mango
4 tbsp red onion, finely chopped
1 level tsp salt
4 tbsp lemon/lime juice, freshly squeezed

First, we bake the kohlrabi. Preheat the oven to 375°F/ 190°C. Bake the kohlrabi for about 30 minutes, until a fork slides in smoothly. Allow it to cool, then peel, and dice into ¼ inch / ½ cm pieces. Instead of peeling, you can cut off the sides to form a large cube, then dice.

Make the ceviche right before you serve it.
Cut the fillets into 1 cm cubes and place in a bowl. Pour the olive oil and coat the fish cubes thoroughly. Add the cilantro and mix together. Mix in the kohlrabi, mango, and red onion. Finally, add the salt and lemon or lime juice and mix.

Israeli Ceviche

Serves 4 as a starter

10 oz / 280 g freshest fillet, skinned and bones removed (amberjack, sea bass or the like)

4 tbsp olive oil

¾ tsp coarse grain sea salt

2 tbsp pomegranate molasses

⅔ cup / 120 g bulgur, soaked in boiling water

3 tbsp dried tomato paste

scant 3 oz / 80 g fresh mint leaves, chopped

scant 3 oz / 80 g fresh cilantro leaves, chopped

⅔ cup / 120 g roasted red peppers or tart mango, cut into thin strips

5 tbsp / 80 g lemon fillet cubes, diced into ¼ inch / ½ cm pieces

4 tbsp tomato, diced into ½ cm pieces

¾ tsp freshly ground allspice

¾ tsp ground coriander seeds

Cut the filets into ½ inch / 1 cm cubes and place in a mixing bowl.

Add the olive oil, and mix well to coat the fish. Add salt and pomegranate molasses.

Mix well.

Remove the bulgur from the water and drain thoroughly.

Knead the bulgur with the dried tomato paste.

Add the bulgur mix with the rest of the ingredients into the mixing bowl and gently mix together.

Saturday Eve Fish Serenade

Some things are not to be argued over: You eat fish on Saturday eve. Now, if you are not fluent in halacha (Jewish law), you might think that means Saturday. However, since the Jewish calendar has sunset marking the start of a new day, Saturday starts on Friday evening. That's the first thing and not to be disputed. The second thing refers to how fish came to be associated with the Sabbath, and that is a bit murkier.

One explanation for fish being eaten on the Sabbath may be that the command to delight in the Sabbath was satisfied by delighting in food and drink, and fish were considered a delight. Another approach looks at the blessing fish were given when God created them on the fifth day. He blessed them to be fruitful and multiply, the same blessing Adam and Eve received on Friday. Adam and Eve's blessing was interpreted to extend into Saturday and since fish had the same blessing, fish were also associated with Saturday. Which, as explained above, begins Friday.

The strongest pro-fish-on-Friday argument for me was that eating fish was a long-standing tradition. So, I joined in. For a typical Friday evening Sabbath meal, we make four different dishes of fish, so all can indulge their own taste.

We have the etched-in-stone baked salmon my mother makes, my sister-in-law's roasted grey mullets, the fish schnitzels I serve for the sake of the grandkids, and the Moroccan fish or sea bass in curry I usually make for my nephews. So, we have four dishes for four generations.

Moroccan Fish

Moroccan Fish

Serves 4

4 tbsp olive oil
2 tbsp paprika
¼ tsp hot paprika
scant tbsp turmeric
¼ tsp cumin (optional)
1½ tsp salt
1 tbsp ground coriander
1½ lb / 700 g white fish fillets, Nile perch, barramundi, tilapia and such, soaked in lemon water for several minutes
1 red pepper, cored and sliced
2 tomatoes, sliced
1 tbsp preserved lemon (optional)
1 red chile pepper, thinly sliced (optional)
12 garlic cloves, halved or sliced lengthwise
½ cup / 70 g cilantro, with stalks, coarsely chopped
1 cup cooked chickpeas (page 106), or use drained can chickpeas)
½ lemon, sliced
2 tbsp freshly squeezed lemon juice

In a medium mixing bowl, mix together olive oil and spices.

Dip the fillets a couple at a time in the spice mix and make sure to coat well.

Layer a sauté pan with half the slices of red pepper and tomatoes, layer the fillets on top, and layer the rest of the red peppers and the preserved lemon, if using.

Layer the chile pepper, garlic, and cilantro and cover with the chickpeas.

Layer the rest of the tomatoes and lemon slices.

Pour water into the mixing bowl and scrape in any spice leftovers, add to the pan to cover the fillets and a bit more.

Bring to a boil, then lower the heat and add the lemon juice.

Cook for ten minutes more.

Fish Kebabs with Preserved Lemon Cream

Serves 4

For the kebabs:

1⅓ lb / 600 g mullet OR grouper, fillet boned and skinned

1¾ oz / 50 g fresh coriander

1¾ oz / 50 g fresh parsley

a few sprigs of fresh mint

1 small onion

7 garlic cloves, peeled

½ tsp ground dried coriander

½ tsp ground cumin

¼ tsp ground cinnamon

¼ tsp ground nutmeg

¼ cup olive oil

1 tsp salt

½ tsp ground black pepper

7 tbsp / 100 ml vegetable oil

For the lemon cream:

2 medium lemons, each cut into 8 pieces

1 cup water

3½ tbsp white vinegar

¼ tsp ground dried coriander

½ tsp ground cumin

⅕ chile pepper

½ tsp salt

½ cup olive oil

To make the kebabs:

In a food processor, grind all the ingredients together, except the vegetable oil, to make a crumbly mixture.

Form kebabs out of the mixture and chill well. Brush with vegetable oil.

Prepare a medium-high 400°F/ 200°C gas or charcoal grill fire. Brush the grill grates with oil several times to ensure a nonstick surface.

Place the fish kebabs on the grill and cook, turning occasionally, until the fish turns opaque, about 10 minutes total.

Remove from the grill. Serve with a dollop of lemon cream.

To make the lemon cream:

Place the lemon and water in a medium saucepan and bring to a boil.

Cook for 15 minutes until the lemons are soft. Allow to cool.

Add the vinegar and spices. Chill for 1 hour and blend well with olive oil to create a smooth cream.

Profiteroles Stuffed with Fish Shawarma

In this recipe, the shawarma is used figuratively – it represents the spice mix of the actual dish of slowly roasting marinated meat stacked on a rotating spit. Traditionally, shawarma is prepared from different meats. It could be lamb, turkey, beef or chicken, but fish is never used, as its flesh is not fatty enough. Nevertheless, we liked the combination of the shawarma spice mix with a white fish. Since it requires a shorter cooking time, we simply sear it with complementary onions and tomatoes.

The baharat spice mix of the shawarma consists of ground turmeric, coriander seeds, cumin, cardamom, paprika, cinnamon, and black pepper. It can be store bought or homemade.

The profiteroles – pastry puffs – replace the flatbread of pita or laffa in the original dish. This seems almost blasphemous, as profiteroles are nearly exclusively eaten filled with vanilla cream and drizzled with hot chocolate fudge. However, the choux pastry has a great airiness to it, so the profiterole lightly soaks up the flavors of the sauce while beautifully wrapping the dish together.

Makes 20 profiteroles

For the profiteroles:

½ cup / 120 ml water

½ cup / 120 ml unsweetened soy milk

½ cup / 110 g butter or 6 tbsp / 90 ml vegetable oil

1 tsp / 6 g sugar

¾ tsp / 4 g salt

1 cup /150 g all-purpose flour

4-5 eggs, beaten

To make the profiteroles:

Preheat the oven to 320°F/ 160°C.

Place all the ingredients, except the flour and eggs, in a heavy based non-stick saucepan. Bring to a simmer on medium heat, occasionally stirring. Once simmering, lower the heat and add the flour, constantly blending in, using a whisk. The mixture should thicken immediately.

When the flour is assimilated and the dough forms a ball, leaving the sides of the saucepan clean, remove from heat. Let it cool for about 5 minutes. While the dough is still warm, add the eggs one at a time, whisking in until completely blended before adding the next egg.

After the fourth egg has been incorporated, check the elasticity of the dough.

The dough should be smooth, glossy and thick, with a consistency of a stretched grilled mozzarella. If the dough is too thick and does not stretch, add the fifth egg.

Transfer the dough to a pastry bag, and line a tray with parchment paper. Pipe 1 inch / 2½ cm diameter mounds about 1¼ inch / 3 cm tall, allowing for 2 inch / 5 cm spaces between them.

Place the tray in the oven, and bake for 20-30 minutes, depending on the oven.

The profiteroles should rise slowly, until more than double their size, but should remain moist. Bake until golden brown.

For the fish shawarma:

2 tbsp olive oil

2 onions, finely chopped

6 tomatoes, seeded and finely diced

7 oz / 200 g white fish fillets, such as grouper or sea bass, diced to about 1 cm cubes

1 tbsp thyme, chopped

1 tbsp shawarma spice mix

salt

freshly ground black pepper

To make the fish shawarma:

Heat the olive oil in a large skillet, and add the onions and tomatoes, stirring until soft and lightly browned.

Take the onions and tomatoes out of the skillet, and add olive oil.

Add the fish and stir until cooked to a crisp.

Return the onions and tomatoes to the skillet, and add the seasonings, mixing well.

Remove from heat.

Build it up:

Cut the profiteroles in half, and pile with a tablespoon of fish shawarma, close it up and pile on a serving plate.

We like to serve them with tahini and amba aioli.

Seared Red Tuna

Serves 4

1⅓ lb / 600 g red tuna fillets, skinned, cut into long strips

For the vinaigrette:

6 tbsp freshly squeezed lemon juice

6½ tbsp / 100 ml olive oil

⅓ red chile pepper, finely chopped

1 oz / 25 g fresh basil, finely chopped

1 orange, squeezed and zested

salt

black pepper

For the couscous:

2 small Roma tomatoes (3½ oz / 100 g in total)

1 tbsp olive oil

sea salt

½ tsp dried thyme leaves

1½ cups / 150 g fine bulgur

1¼ cup / 300 ml boiling vegetable stock

1 small eggplant (about 7 oz / 200 g)

¾ cup / 200 ml vegetable oil for frying

⅓ cup / 50 g pine nuts

½ tbsp capers in brine

½ tbsp orange zest

½ tbsp lemon zest

black pepper

Preheat the oven to 250°F / 120°C.
Peel the tomatoes, quarter them and empty out the seeds.
Place the tomatoes on a baking sheet lined with parchment paper.
Sprinkle with olive oil, sea salt, and thyme and dry in the oven until deep red and slightly shriveled, about an hour.
Remove from the oven and let the tomatoes cool enough to handle. Chop roughly.

Lightly fry bulgur in olive oil and the soak the bulgur in the hot stock, covered, until al dente. Fluff it up with a spoon.
Dice the eggplant into small cubes – about ¼ inch / ½ cm – and deep fry until golden brown.
Heat a medium pan on medium heat and sauté the pine nuts until golden, stirring for about 3 minutes. Remove from the pan and set aside to cool.

Wash the capers well from salt and fry in the same pan until slightly crispy.
Combine the bulgur with the tomatoes and eggplants, add the pine nuts, capers and lightly mix with the zest of the oranges and lemons.
There are two options to sear the tuna strips:
Sear on a grill for about a minute for each side. Or, heat a skillet over medium-high heat for about 2-3 minutes before searing the strips of tuna about a minute each side, so that they are still rare inside. Set aside to cool.
Blend the ingredients for the vinaigrette together to a smooth consistency – season it well.
Before serving, slice the tuna thinly and drizzle with the vinaigrette.

To serve, spoon the couscous onto serving dishes, and place the tuna strips on top.

Sweets

Almond Milk Malabi

Ice from Paradise

As a soldier on the Egyptian frontier in the Sinai Peninsula, I had the privilege to view the remains of a Greek temple located amidst salt marshes. The pudding described in this recipe is an opaque white and indeed resembles the salt marshes. Those marshes or mud gave the City of Pelusium, or The City of Mud, its ancient name, and consequently this dessert's original name, balouza, the Arabic pronunciation of Pelusium.

I was always intrigued by the way the ancient world is portrayed in hidden gems in our current, everyday life. The tell-tale signs remain in the names of places, foods, and of everyday objects, but for most people the origin is long forgotten. Balouza is a perfect example.

This dessert was adapted from a balouza recipe by Claudia Roden. Balouza (aka Pelusium, the City of Mud) was an ancient Greek city on the eastern bank of the Nile, where linen (linum Pelusiacum) was the principal product. The word *blouse* is derived from the Arabic pronunciation of the Pelusian shirt.

It is also mentioned in the Mishna that the high priest wore pilusin – the best linen. One day I heard a shout in the dining room of the restaurant, *Yaacht behasht!* An American of Persian descent was calling out the Persian name in tears. She said it brought back the memory of her grandmother who used to prepare this dessert. In Persian, it is called *ice from paradise.*

Serves 6

For the pudding:

½ cup / 60 g cornstarch

3 cups / 750 ml almond milk (store bought or see recipe, page 222)

½ cup / 120 g sugar

3 drops rose water

6 tbsp / 90 ml water

For the syrup:

⅔ cup / 140 ml water

¾ cup / 140 g sugar

¾ cup dried hibiscus flowers, can be replaced with strawberry coulis

To make the pudding:

Combine the cornstarch with 6¾ tbsp / 100 ml of the almond milk and stir to a smooth paste.

Pour the remaining almond milk into a medium saucepan and add the sugar, rose water, and water.

Simmer on low heat and whisk to dissolve the sugar.

Add the cornstarch mixture to the saucepan while stirring constantly, and bring to a boil. The mixture should thicken to a point that when a spoon is dipped, the pudding coat clings on. Remove from heat and pour into dessert cups.

Place in the fridge for at least 2 hours.

To make the syrup:

Place the water, sugar, and hibiscus flowers in a small saucepan.

Bring to a boil while stirring to dissolve the sugar. Reduce heat and cook for about 5 minutes.

Chill and pass through a sieve.

To serve, drizzle the syrup on top of the pudding.

Poached Pears

The desserts in kosher restaurants that serve meat used to be looked down upon. That was due to both a perception that dairy makes the best desserts, and to the notorious non-dairy whipped cream, with its very distinctive texture and flavor, used in the Eighties to make the pareve chocolate mousse.

Back in those days, to avoid that artificial flavor, it was easier to use genuine fruit for a *plant-based* dessert. The poached pears were a fantastic option. They were easy to make, could be cooked in advance, and if anything, the chilling time actually enhanced their flavor. They were the natural choice!

As the vegan movement becomes much more prevalent, the conception of desserts is changing. Serious pastry chefs are altering the paradigm. They are bringing new plant-based ingredients to the level of the proper, if not exquisite, dessert.

In homage to the original plant-based dessert, we offer you the poached pear. That dessert accompanied us to all the restaurant's locations and through all its incarnations. In the last several years, we added a dollop of almond cream that accents the firmness and sweetness of the pears and showcases the versatility and ingenuity of the up-and-coming vegan choices. It does not seek to simulate that elusive dairy flavor, but to create a fine almond texture and rich essence.

Serves 6

6 pears (about 2 lb / 1 kg in total), peeled and whole
1¾ cups / 350 g sugar
3 cups / 750 ml red wine
2 cinnamon sticks
½ cup dried hibiscus, optional
water

Place the pears in a saucepan with the sugar, red wine, cinnamon sticks, hibiscus if using, and water to cover. Bring to a boil.

Reduce the heat, and simmer, for about 30 minutes, until a fork slides in easily.

Remove the pears, and continue to reduce the syrup to a runny consistency.

Refrigerate the pears and serve cold.

Place a pear on each serving plate and pour some syrup over it. We serve the pears with a dollop of almond cream.

Almond Vanilla Cream

14 oz / 400 g blanched almonds
1 cup water
6 tbsp soy cream
⅔ tsp vanilla extract
2 tbsp sugar

Place the almonds and water in a food processor bowl and soak for about 30 minutes. Add the soy cream, vanilla extract and sugar, and process for about 3-4 minutes until a uniform texture is achieved. Store in an air-tight container for up to 3 days.

Forever Chocolate

There is an unequivocal ranking of chocolate that places it at the top of best-desserts charts. It is certainly an ingredient that attracts most people. In the restaurant, we strive to orchestrate the finest dining experience for our guests, making the final note a sweet one.

These recipes are all about being a kosher restaurant yet wishing to serve that elusive best chocolate-y dessert for the followers of the cocoa bean. We look for desserts that are based on dark chocolate, since it is pareve, then substitute butter with cocoa butter, which is pareve as well. The truffles, which follow this recipe, have condensed chocolate textures, while the chocolate souffle, like a journey cut short, aims at a molten quality rather than that of a proper chocolate cake. If your sweet tooth is chocolate-inclined – like that of 90 percent of the population – it will be well taken care of by this and the next recipes.

Chocolate Souffle

For best results, run a test bake for one of the souffles: To identify the ideal baking time, test readiness after 10 minutes with the jiggle test.

Serves 4-6 depending on dish size

4 tbsp / 60 g cocoa butter
4 oz / 110 g dark chocolate, coarsely chopped
3 large free-range eggs
1 tsp pure vanilla extract
3 tbsp / 40 g sugar
3 tbsp / 45 g chickpea flour, or all-purpose flour

Melt the cocoa butter and the dark chocolate together in a double boiler or in a large glass bowl in the microwave. If using the microwave, do it in increments of 30 seconds, stirring after each increment until completely melted and combined. Set aside to cool for 3-5 minutes. Add the eggs, one at a time, whisking well until combined. Add the vanilla extract and sugar and blend. Finally add the chickpea flour and blend just until combined. Place the batter in the refrigerator for 10 minutes. Adjust the oven rack to the lower third position and preheat to 350°F / 180°C. Brush oven-safe straight sided ramekins with a coating of oil. Spoon batter evenly into the ramekins, filling about ¾ of the dish. Using a knife or spatula, smooth down the surface. Place the ramekins on a baking sheet and place into the oven. Bake for 10-12 minutes or until the edges are set and the center just barely moves when you give the pan a light jiggle. Remove from the oven and serve immediately.

Chocolate Truffles

Yields about 24 truffles

10½ oz / 300 g dark chocolate, finely chopped, or use chocolate chips

⅔ cup / 150 ml soy cream

½ tsp vanilla extract

Variation:

½ cup plus 1 tbsp / 75 g whole almonds

1 tsp brown sugar

⅛ tsp salt

Topping:

unsweetened cocoa powder

Place the chocolate in a heat proof bowl.

Heat the soy cream until it is simmering on the stovetop or in the microwave. If using the microwave, heat in 20 seconds increments to avoid boiling the cream.

Immediately pour the simmering cream on the chocolate.

Allow the cream to sit a minute before vigorously stirring the chocolate cream mixture to thoroughly melt the chocolate.

Add the vanilla extract and stir well. If the chocolate hasn't completely melted, heat the bowl in the microwave for another 20 seconds, then stir to combine.

If adding the almonds, place the almonds in a small saucepan on medium heat and roast for about 3-4 minutes until golden brown.
Add the sugar and a sprinkle of salt and allow the sugar to dissolve and coat the almonds. Remove from heat and place into a bowl. Using a meat mallet, break the clusters of almonds into pieces.
Add the caramelized almonds to the chocolate ganache and mix.

Spread the chocolate ganache into a shallow dish and cover. Refrigerate for 3-4 hours or overnight.

Place 2 tablespoons of cocoa powder in a medium container and spread evenly.
There are 2 options to form the truffles. For the lazy option, cut the chilled truffles mixture criss-cross into 1½×¾ inch / 4×2 cm pieces.
To form truffle balls (the non-lazy method), scoop 2 teaspoon servings and roll each into a ball.
Roll the truffle balls or rectangles into the cocoa powder box and jiggle gently to cover.
Remove and set aside.
Place into an airtight container and refrigerate until serving.

Aunt Aliza's Baklava

Sweets in Iraq

Before they left Iraq, my family, the Basson's, had a factory in Amara that produced sesame oil and raw tahini. During the Jewish holidays, the factory also made customary sweets. One such sweet was *hadgi badam* – coconut cookies topped with an almond – the same cookies made for Passover because they are flourless. Another was *mann-al-sama* – a specialty marshmallow-like nougat with nuts. The same custom of making the confections on Jewish holidays traveled to Israel with my family and into the family bakery, which also produced *massapan* (almond marzipan), baklava, and *luzina* (quince candies). My aunts would set up booths, displaying the confections for sale.

In their great ovens, they would bake the baklava, the crisp and nutty pastry, spiced with cardamom in the Iraqi version. Our baklava is mild on sugar, and the cardamom contributes to the richness of flavors. Traditionally, the preparation of filo pastry required considerable skill and was done by hand; however, currently the filo dough may be bought frozen or chilled in most supermarkets.

Though the abundance of confections would seem to have been enough to satisfy every kid's sweet tooth, the dessert that keeps my mother reminiscing is the fresh head of lettuce her father used to distribute among the kids.

Yields about 40 baklavas

For the syrup:

1½ cup sugar

1 cup water

3 tbsp lemon juice

10 drops orange blossom water, optional

For the topping:

½ cup crushed pistachios to garnish

For the filling:

2 cups / 240 g unsalted pistachios

1 cup / 100 g almonds

1 cup / 100 g walnuts

2 tbsp brown sugar

scant 1 tbsp ground cardamom

1 lb / 500 g filo pastry sheets, if frozen, thawed in the fridge the night before

1 cup / 200 g melted butter / sunflower oil

To make the syrup:

Place the sugar and water in a small saucepan and bring to a light simmer, stir using a wooden spoon to dissolve the sugar. Add the lemon juice and orange blossom water, stir and remove from heat. Allow to cool.

To make and add the filling:

In a food processor, pulse the pistachios, almonds, and walnuts to a coarsely chopped texture, transfer to a large mixing bowl and add the brown sugar and ground cardamom, mixing well.

Preheat the oven to 400°F / 200°C.

To keep the filo pastry moist while preparing the baklava, cover the remaining dough using a clean kitchen towel.

Brush a 9×13 inch / 23×33 cm baking pan with some of the melted butter or oil.

Place a filo square in the pan and brush it thoroughly with melted butter / oil. Repeat with 10 sheets.

Evenly spread the nut mixture on the filo sheet, and top with 10 more sheets of filo, brushing each one with melted butter/ oil before topping with the next.

Using a sharp knife cut a diagonal cut from one corner of the pan to the other. Repeat in 1½ inch / 4 cm spaces. Then cut straight lines lengthwise to form diamond shaped pieces.

Brush with the remaining melted butter/ oil when done.

Bake for 25 minutes until golden and crisp.

Immediately after taking the baklava out of the oven, pour the cooled syrup slowly over it.

Sprinkle with the chopped pistachios.

Song of Songs Cake

Flowing with Milk and Honey

This cake is basically an apple cake. However, it is not mere coincidence that made it my grandson's favorite cake. Nor, is it by coincidence that it is the only cake he fervently asks for on birthdays or holidays, and from which he happily takes home leftovers to fight over with his sister.

Apple cakes inherently encompass comfort: Refresh me with raisin cakes, Sustain me with apples, Because I am lovesick. Song of Songs 2:5.

The age-old coupling with cinnamon, doesn't seem like a mere coincidence either: Nard and saffron, calamus and cinnamon, with every kind of incense tree, with myrrh and aloes and all the finest spices. Song of Songs 4:14.

Cinnamon was used as a means to show off wealth and was considered a gift fit for kings. Studies have shown that it has high concentrations of antioxidants and anti-inflammatory compounds, which contribute to its status as a medicinal plant. That provides at least part of the rationale for the popularity of this commodity since the Portuguese started shipping it to Europe in the fifteenth century. When baked together, the cinnamon enhances the natural sweetness of the apples, allowing us to reduce sugar amounts.

The cake recipe is a family adaptation of the Rina Valero version found in *Delights of Jerusalem* – a magnificent cookbook that collects a variety of recipes from Jerusalem mothers who follow the Jewish, Muslim, and Christian faiths, and curates their stories and their spirits. For the restaurant, we need it to be pareve – not dairy – so we opted for the use of orange juice and oil.

Serves 10–12

¾ cup + 2 tbsp / 200 g unsalted butter at room temperature OR ⅔ cup /160 ml vegetable oil
1 cup brown sugar
2 free-range eggs
1 tsp vanilla extract
2 cups flour
½ tsp baking soda
2 tsp baking powder
1 cup orange juice OR 1 cup buttermilk
5 Granny Smith apples (1¾ lb / 800 g in total), peeled and diced ⅔ inch / 1.5 cm, cores removed
6 tbsp brown sugar
2 tsp cinnamon

Preheat the oven to 350°F / 180°C.
In a large bowl, cream together the butter and sugar until light and fluffy.
Add the eggs 1 at a time, beating well with each addition, then stir in the vanilla.
Combine the flour with the baking soda and baking powder.
Add the flour mixture alternately with the orange juice; beat well.

Place the apples in a medium bowl and sprinkle with 3 tablespoons of sugar, and 1 teaspoon cinnamon, combine.

Grease a 10 inch / 26 cm springform pan with butter or oil.
Pour half the batter into the pan and level it, using a spatula.
Cover the batter with an even layer of apple mixture.
Pour the remaining cake batter over the apples.
Sprinkle the batter with remaining sugar and cinnamon.
Bake for 45 minutes.

Tanned Quince

Some ingredients enchant me, seemingly magical in their power to unlock a secret path to my memories and imagination. Figs bring up memories of my childhood, of climbing the fig tree to get to its hidden flowers' fruit. The sweet scent of quince reminds me of caramelizing quince jam, slowly cooking on the stovetop, with the promise of a delightful confection and strong black tea.

Quince is the ultimate fruit for canned preserves. Consequently, marmalade, which is synonymous with jam and jellies, derived from *marmelo* – quince in Portuguese. Too tart to be eaten raw, and full of pectic, which makes it so well preserved when cooked, quince was the first fruit to be made into jam.

I love cooking with quince and am dismayed that quince suffers from being somewhat collectively unfashionable. When I add them to any slow-cooked dish from the savory to confections, they add richness of taste that complements the flavor and textures.

On holidays, in Iraq, they used to make quince *luzina* – which is essentially jam that was rolled out and cut into fudge-like candies, sometimes mixed with nuts or coconut and flavored with rose water. This quince dessert recipe resembles confiture rather than a proper jam and would be greatly enriched with a dollop of cream or vanilla ice cream.

Serve with freshly brewed strong fragrant black tea.

Serves 4

2-3 quinces (1 lb / 500 g in total), peeled and quartered, cores removed

¾ cup / 150 g sugar

1 cup red wine

2 whole cloves

water

Place the quince quarters and cores in a saucepan with the sugar, red wine, cloves, and water to cover. Bring to a boil and keep boiling for 10 minutes. Ladle off the foam from the surface.

Reduce the heat, and continue to cook, simmering, for at least an hour, until the quince are soft and their color becomes deep red.

Remove the cooked quince from the saucepan and set aside. Discard the cores. Continue to cook the sauce until reduced to a syrup-like consistency.

Place 2 quince quarters on each serving plate and drizzle some syrup over it.

Goes great with vanilla ice cream and almond cream.

Cocktails

Eucalyptus Moonshine

When we travelled to Italy on our honeymoon, Maya and I visited a friend of ours from Jerusalem that was staying in Naples at the time, a philosophy lecturer. His family was staying in the former servant quarters of an estate, and the owners invited all of us to their Sunday lunch.

The meal was an extravagant one. The owners had seven daughters, each in turn presented her dish, which included *spaghetti alle vongole*, a wide variety of pasta, followed by dessert platters of cheese and bologna, a delectable *torta caprese*, an endless ensemble of dishes and fragrances. Along with the desserts, they served a digestif, Strega liqueur, native to the nearby city of Benevento.

The Strega liqueur is traditionally made from 70 different varieties of herbs, and legend has it that its recipe was given to a family by witches, hence giving the liqueur its name – strega means a witch in Italian. Whether it was witchcraft of Benevento or simply a smart blend, the digestif worked magic. We bought a bottle to take back with us.

A decade later, we had quite a few frequent diners-turned-friends whose families were based in Italy, and we shared a love for the Strega liqueur. They would bring me back a bottle every time they visited Italy. I shared this digestif with my friends from the Italian community, until I felt I should look for a local replacement.

I started infusing dried sticks of licorice root in arak bottles. Arak is an alcoholic drink made from grapes and anise seeds, and the addition of the licorice highlighted the anise flavors and turned the liquid from clear to golden. We began serving our concoction in the restaurant as a digestif and later we developed other herbal and fruit liqueurs, such as geranium and quince. At times we even sold them in the restaurant to digestif enthusiasts.

Arak with Passion Fruit

Serves 1

1 tsp hibiscus powder, optional

2 oz / 60 ml arak

5 tsp / 25 ml passion fruit syrup

3 tsp / 15 ml freshly squeezed lemon juice

½ large egg white

Rim the glass (optional) as follows: Fill a small plate with hibiscus powder. Moisten a paper towel and wipe it along the outside of the rim of a martini glass. Invert the glass and dip the rim until it is covered with a thin ring of hibiscus powder. Set aside.

In a shaker with no ice, add all the ingredients. Dry shake (without ice) vigorously for 30 seconds, to allow the egg white to foam.

Add ice to the shaker and shake for about 30 seconds to chill the cocktail.

Strain and pour into the hibiscus-rimmed martini glass.

Smoky Tamarind

Serves 1

lime or lemon wedge

salt

¾ oz / 20 ml tamarind concentrate

¼ oz / 10 ml simple sugar syrup

½ large egg white

2 oz / 60 ml mezcal

1 oz / 30 ml freshly squeezed orange juice

1 oz / 30 ml allspice syrup

Salt the rim (optional) as follows: Fill a small plate with salt. Run the juicy side of a lime wedge around the outside top rim of a tulip glass. Dip the rim until it is covered with a thin ring of salt. Set aside.

Mix the tamarind concentrate with the sugar syrup to combine.

In a shaker with no ice, add all the ingredients. Dry shake (without ice) vigorously for 30 seconds, to allow the egg white to foam.

Add ice to the shaker and shake for about 30 seconds to chill the cocktail.

Strain and pour into the salted rimmed tulip glass.

For the simple sugar syrup:

1 cup white sugar

1 cup water

To make the simple sugar syrup:

Combine the sugar and water in a small saucepan over medium heat until the sugar dissolves. Bring to a boil, then remove from heat, and leave to cool. Bottle for future use. This stores in the refrigerator for up to a month.

For the allspice syrup:

¾ oz / 20 g whole allspice berries

¾ cup / 150 g sugar

2 cups / 500 ml water

To make the allspice syrup:

Cook the allspice berries, sugar, and water in a small saucepan over low heat until the sugar dissolves.

Bring to a boil, then remove from heat, and leave to cool. Bottle for future use. This stores in the fridge for up to a month.

Jerusalem Mule

Serves 1

4 tsp / 20 ml lemon vodka

4 tsp / 20 ml vodka

10 tsp / 50 ml quince vodka

3 tsp / 15 ml freshly squeezed lemon juice

3 tsp / 15 ml simple sugar syrup

¼ oz / 10 ml cardamom vodka

1 oz / 30 m ginger beer

Pour all the ingredients into a copper mug. Add ice cubes and stir to combine.

For the quince vodka:

1 medium quince

26⅓ oz / 750 ml vodka

To make the quince vodka:

Peel, seed, and chop the quince.

Add the quince pieces to a large jar, then add the vodka.

Cover and allow to rest in a cool, dark place for 7 days. When ready to use, remove and discard the quince pieces.

For the cardamom vodka:

2 tbsp cardamom pods, slightly cracked

26⅓ oz / 750 ml vodka

Add the cardamom pods to a large jar, then add the vodka. Cover and allow to rest in a cool, dark place for 7 days. When ready to use, strain and discard the cardamom pods.

Jerusalem Sangria

Serves 1

3⅓ oz / 100 ml red wine

3 tsp / 15 ml freshly squeezed lemon juice

5 tsp / 25 ml passion fruit syrup

1 oz / 30 ml white rum

2 sage leaves, roughly torn

Fill the shaker with all the ingredients.

Add ice to the shaker, just above the level of the liquid, and shake for about 30 seconds to chill the cocktail.

Strain and pour into a martini glass.

The Rose Garden

Serves 1

1 tsp sugar

½ tsp cinnamon

1⅓ oz / 40 ml Campari

2⅓ oz / 70 ml vodka

5 tsp / 25 ml freshly squeezed lemon juice

5 tsp / 25 ml simple sugar syrup

3 tsp / 15 ml rose water

Rim the glass (optional) as follows: Fill a small plate with sugar and cinnamon and mix them together. Moisten a paper towel and wipe it along the outside rim of a small tulip glass to moisten the glass. Dip the glass, rim down into the sugar mixture until it is covered with a thin ring of sugar and cinnamon. Set aside.

Fill the shaker with all the ingredients.
Add ice to the shaker, just above the level of the liquid, and shake for about 30 seconds to chill the cocktail.
Strain and pour into the sugar-rimmed tulip glass.

Condiments and Basics

Pickled Cucumbers

In the past couple of years, we have been making our own pickled cucumbers.

It began when Sharon, my daughter, tried a recipe from a blog she was following. Starting out, she used the one-quart jar. It was consumed so quickly that she doubled the amount, and then she tripled it.

When you make your own pickles in brine, amidst assets such as flavor and satisfying crunch, there is one prime benefit – friendly bacteria thrive in the fermentation process and, when eaten, act as a probiotic supplement. Recently, a great deal of research has focused on gut microbiomes and their relationship to eating food rich in probiotics. Studies are finding that when we eat probiotic-rich food, such as the pickled cucumbers in this recipe, we boost our gut bacteria, which helps with digestion, with immune function, with the absorption of nutrients, and even influences our brain function and mental health. Supermarket pickles, including the ones without vinegar, are pasteurized and thus have no probiotics.

Makes a 3 quart / 3 liter jar

5 cups / 1½ liters water
5 tsp salt
2 ¾ lb / 1⅓ kg cucumbers, fresh and firm
2 oz / 60 g fresh dill
3 large garlic cloves
15 black peppercorns
8 allspice berries

Bring the water and salt to a boil in a large saucepan, blend to dissolve the salt, remove from heat, let cool.

Wash the cucumbers and dill thoroughly. Remove any blossoms.

Sterilize a 3 quart / 3 liter jar. Align the cucumbers vertically in the bottom of the jar and place half the dill with the bottom pile.

Peel and vertically cut the garlic into thick slices. Slide in the garlic slices, half the peppercorns, and the allspice berries between the cucumbers.

Align another layer of cucumbers, gently pressing them, so they fit tightly together.

Add another batch of dill, followed by the spices.

Fill the jar with the salt water. The cucumbers should be completely covered.

Seal the canning jar with a fitted lid. In the first 3 days, some brine might spill over, so it is advisable to keep the jar on a large plate.

Leave to ferment for 7 days.

Berrak
נתרן
בכמות גבוהה
חצילים
קלויים ומוחמצים
Roasted Eggplant

The Wandering Jew

In a hidden passage created in the Early Middle Ages, we can find remnants of a guild of Jewish merchants – the Radhanites. They travelled along the silk routes, speaking various languages – Arabic, Persian, Roman, Old French, and Slavic – carrying their goods on camelback all the way to Suez. By ship, they sailed to France and back again.

This special guild was established as a result of early clashes between emerging Muslim polities and the Christian kingdoms of Europe; the mutual ban of each other's goods allowed the Radhanites to flourish as a neutral go-between and to establish a virtual monopoly in merchant trade. Consequently, the Radhanites were among the first to connect the trade routes from Western Europe to Eastern Asia.

Some scholars believe that the Radhanites were instrumental to the establishment of Jewish communities along the route. They may have been forerunners of the banking system due to their use of letters of credit to avoid carrying large quantities of money and being targeted for theft.

Among the luxury merchandise they carried were intricate weapons, jewelry, silk, and fur. Our predominant cargo of interest were the spices they carried in small, yet pricey sacks. Spices such as cinnamon, cardamom, ginger, pepper, turmeric,

nutmeg, and cloves were brought from the Far East to the tables of Europe.

The disappearance of the Radhanites may be linked to the fall of Tang dynasty in China and the later collapse of Khazarian Turks, causing trade routes to become unsafe. The rise of Italian city-states and their takeover of the trade was also associated with the disappearance of the Radhanites. When they halted trade, a profound void was created: spices disappeared from Europe's 10th-century kitchens.

Iraqi Tbit Baharat Spice Mix

1 oz / 30 g whole allspice berries

1 oz / 30 g cinnamon bark

⅓ oz / 10 g cardamom pods (about 18)

⅔ oz / 20 g nutmeg seeds (about 3)

Crush the cinnamon and nutmeg to medium pieces using a mortar and pestle. Place the ingredients in a spice grinder and grind to a fine powder.

Best reserved in a glass jar in the freezer.

Index

Q

R

S

T

Acknowledgments

This book was born out of the universal love for food and the fundamental expression of love through food. The effort was synergetic. Moshe had the recipes, the restaurant, the lore, and the tradition. Sharon took all that and more, and turned a dream into words and tales, shining and glossy on the printed page. The first thanks in this book are therefore from Moshe and Sharon to one another. Then, from our hearts, we thank those many unnamed people and a few named individuals, without whom this book couldn't have come to life.

Above all, we are grateful to Ofer Levin for supporting this creation with the altruistic purpose of promoting Israeli culture, and for your great investment in helping us realize our aspiration. Magen Halutz, you formed this cookbook and brought it to fruition. Your patience and vision are evident on every page. Thank you for making this dream come true. Renee Atlas, our editor, thank you for your meticulous and literary work to ensure we come up with more than the sum of our ingredients. Your honest enthusiasm is greatly appreciated. Our photographers, Or Doga, Steve Ryan, Ricky Rachman, Lior Basson, and Elad Sarig, thank you for pairing your great talent with enormous hearts. Every shot is a source of pride and joy.

We both thank as well, those who have given their good names, renown, and accomplishments to support this book. Michael Solomonov, Gil Hovav, and Art Smith, your valued perceptions guided us. Likewise, we thank Yossi Klein Halevi for your generous spirit, for sharing your vast literary experience, and above all, for your genuine friendship.

We thank the talented Rose Levy Beranbaum, whose soul creates the sweetness of her recipes. You've been with us at every step, giving us unmitigated support through the challenge of publishing. For the one and only Claudia Roden, thank you for being a brilliant inspiration, and valued friend. We, like the

world, cannot imagine Jewish cooking without your pioneering curating and creativity.

Each of us wants to thank a few people who added special flavor to this cookbook.

From Moshe:
The staff of The Eucalyptus are my second family. Such a stressful environment creates strong connections! We are particularly lucky to have been working with many of our staff for so long. Michal Samuels-Korenman, thank you for your eternal optimism and enthusiasm, your contribution is worth more than its weight in gold. Sharbel Ishaq, you take so much of the pressure off every day, thank you for your solid energy and generous heart.

So many people have encouraged me on the path to this book and given me their good counsel: Gamze Ineceli, Rosie Schwartz, Levana Kirschenbaum, Deborah Roberts, Efrem Harkham, Meera Freeman, Jay and Georganne Nixon, and Deborah Harris. A special thanks to chef Shalom Kadosh, the founding father of Israeli cuisine. Your guts, example, and encouragement have paved The Eucalyptus's way. In loving memory of Meredith Farnan: I recall the wonderful hours spent in conversation on your porch in Kansas City.

We are blessed with a family that loves spending time together. In a way, this book is a celebration of those joyous gatherings. I thank my wonderful sister Yaffa, who hosts Friday night dinners and the huge holiday feasts with grace and generosity. I thank my dear brother Yaacov, my early partner and serendipitous mentor who invited me into the restaurant business. I'm always grateful for your solid-as-a-rock love and support.

I extend my gratitude to the many mothers and grandmothers who inhabit and have inhabited my family and the markets and villages that I have known. And the late Zainab Salman of Beit Tsafafa, Vered Eitan of Jerusalem, Abu Abdalla of Battir, and Ahmed Bilbessi of Jerusalem – all of you, my teachers.

I take so much pride in having my kids alongside me in the restaurant and in the production of this project, Sharon, Lior, and Ronny – the fruit of our family tree.

More than words can say, I thank my parents, Spirons and the late Salman Basson, who gave me life and instilled in me the foundation of everything I hold dear – a strong family whose love and support go above and beyond, to eternity and back again.

From Sharon:
This long journey would have been lonely at times, but for our generous community that lent happiness and comfort at each step. I give special thanks to:

Michal Samuels-Korenman – for being a constant resource and a gentle guide for what does and does not work.

Marissa Gross – for always giving me your time, honest opinion, and diligent support.

Sally Ekus – when our ship was heading out of the harbor, you helped us find our North Star; and Deborah Roberts – for generously sharing your profound experience and sensitive advice.

My family is my rock. My parents, Moshe Basson and Maya Basson-Ziv, thank you for teaching me to appreciate the best things in life: love, creativity, laughter, and food. Our kids, Orian, Tom and Amit, thank you for showing me that love is indeed infinite. And most of all, Mike Fradis, my partner, and counterpart, thank you for your endless love and support. You are an inspiration and a fountain of strength.

משק
אחיה
שמן
זית

האקליפטוס
The Eucalyptus
Chef Moshe Basson